Technologies and African Societies in Pandemic Times

*To my friends and colleagues Alain Diassé and Celestin Gnonzion
who passed away too soon*
Julien Atchoua

*To my wife Laetitia, my daughter Jessica and my son Ethan
and all my colleagues and friends*
Jean-Jacques Maomra Bogui

*To my wife Faby and my son Eja and to those who
derive their happiness from serving others*
Saikou Diallo

Africa Digital Age Set

coordinated by
Jean-Paul Bourrières

Volume 2

Technologies and African Societies in Pandemic Times

Using Technology to Survive and Thrive During the Covid-19 Era

Edited by

Saikou Diallo
Jean-Jacques Maomra Bogui
Julien Atchoua

WILEY

First published 2023 in Great Britain and the United States by ISTE Ltd and John Wiley & Sons, Inc.

Apart from any fair dealing for the purposes of research or private study, or criticism or review, as permitted under the Copyright, Designs and Patents Act 1988, this publication may only be reproduced, stored or transmitted, in any form or by any means, with the prior permission in writing of the publishers, or in the case of reprographic reproduction in accordance with the terms and licenses issued by the CLA. Enquiries concerning reproduction outside these terms should be sent to the publishers at the undermentioned address:

ISTE Ltd
27-37 St George's Road
London SW19 4EU
UK

www.iste.co.uk

John Wiley & Sons, Inc.
111 River Street
Hoboken, NJ 07030
USA

www.wiley.com

© ISTE Ltd 2023

The rights of Saikou Diallo, Jean-Jacques Maomra Bogui and Julien Atchoua to be identified as the authors of this work have been asserted by them in accordance with the Copyright, Designs and Patents Act 1988.

Any opinions, findings, and conclusions or recommendations expressed in this material are those of the author(s), contributor(s) or editor(s) and do not necessarily reflect the views of ISTE Group.

Library of Congress Control Number: 2023930940

British Library Cataloguing-in-Publication Data
A CIP record for this book is available from the British Library
ISBN 978-1-78630-452-0

Contents

Foreword xi
Mohamed SALIOU CAMARA

Introduction xv
Jean-Jacques Maomra BOGUI and Nanga Désiré COULIBALY

Part 1. Covid-19, Information, and Communication 1

**Chapter 1. Reinventing Everyday Life in the Covid-19 Era:
The Uses of Information and Communication Technologies
as Tactics in an Abidjanese "Ordinary Courtyard"** 3
Youssouf SOUMAHORO

   1.1. Introduction. 3
      1.1.1. Context and positioning of the research problem 3
      1.1.2. Field and methods 5
   1.2. Results. 6
      1.2.1. Social relational uses. 6
      1.2.2. Hedonic and playful uses 8
      1.2.3. Emerging from the inactivity brought about by the pandemic . . . 9
      1.2.4. Uses for information retrieval and educational purposes. 10
   1.3. Conclusion 12
   1.4. References 13

Chapter 2. Ambivalence of the Use of Digital Technologies in Public Communication About the Pandemic in Côte d'Ivoire 15
Nanga Désiré COULIBALY

2.1. Introduction: Ivorian context of digital technology use in the Covid-19 period 15
    2.1.1. Literature and defining the Covid-19 problem in the Ivorian context 17
    2.1.2. Objectives and research questions 18
2.2. Conceptualization of the social uses of technology in public communication 19
2.3. Collection and method for analyzing ambivalent uses of digital social media in the face of Covid-19 in Côte d'Ivoire 21
2.4. Digital social media, a popular source of information about the pandemic and a source of rumors and miscommunication 22
    2.4.1. Digital social media, the preferred source of information 22
    2.4.2. Rumors and fake news on digital social media, a remedy for miscommunication 26
2.5. Conclusion: understanding the ambivalence of digital social media use in times of Covid-19 27
2.6. References 30

Chapter 3. Fake News and Anti-Covid-19 Vaccines: Analysis of Facebook Users in Burkina Faso 33
Marcel BAGARE

3.1. Introduction 33
3.2. Methodology 36
3.3. The profiles of Facebook users and their content 37
3.4. Fake news in the representation of vaccine risks 43
    3.4.1. The Covid-19 vaccine makes women infertile 44
    3.4.2. Covid vaccines cause neurodegenerative diseases 46
    3.4.3. Bill Gates and his geo-tagged vaccine against Covid 47
3.5. Facebook users confront the vaccine communication strategy and fake news 49
3.6. Conclusion 52
3.7. References 53

Part 2. Covid, Art and Culture 59

Chapter 4. Covid-19 Crisis and Musical Creation for Public Awareness in Africa 61
Julien ATCHOUA

    4.1. Introduction: musical creation for prevention. 61
        4.1.1. Music as a support mechanism and collective commitment 61
        4.1.2. Covid-19, a reality in Africa 62
        4.1.3. The fundamental questions 64
    4.2. Musical information and the Covid-19 crisis in Africa:
collecting and deciphering content. 65
        4.2.1. Objective of the approach 65
        4.2.2. Review and analysis of the corpus. 65
    4.3. Musical works for health prevention 67
        4.3.1. Health awareness and music creation in Africa 67
        4.3.2. Music as a medium for raising health awareness 68
        4.3.3. The issue of health governance in creating music. 71
    4.4. Conclusion 74
        4.4.1. The Covid-19 crisis in Africa: a prevention emergency 74
        4.4.2. Music as a communication medium for health. 74
    4.5. References 76

Chapter 5. Rethinking Theatrical Performances in the Covid-19 Era: Strategies and Perspectives 79
Losséni FANNY

    5.1. Introduction. 79
    5.2. Brief status of Ivorian theatrical performances before Covid-19 81
        5.2.1. The glory years of theatrical performances. 81
        5.2.2. Theatrical performances facing difficulties. 82
    5.3. The situation of theatrical performances during Covid-19 84
        5.3.1. The negative effects of Covid-19 on theatrical performances 84
        5.3.2. Positive effects of Covid-19 on theatrical performances 86
    5.4. Theatrical representations: resilience and resistance. 88
        5.4.1. Theatrical performances as a source of social resilience
during Covid-19 88
        5.4.2. Prospects for theater in situations of a health crisis 91
    5.5. Conclusion 92
    5.6. References 93

Chapter 6. Tourism and the Pandemic: How to be Resilient and Creative Thanks to NICTs. Case study: Aloha Surf Camp in Morocco 95
Hanane MABROUK and John VAN DEN PLAS

6.1. Introduction. 95
6.2. Research methodology 97
    6.2.1. Field surveys using ethnographic and sociological methods. 97
    6.2.2. Research scope 99
6.3. Some geographical, economical and cultural notions of
Moroccan surf tourism. 100
    6.3.1. Tourism in Morocco 101
    6.3.2. The Bay of Taghazout: a flagship destination for "surf"
    and "luxury" tourism. 101
    6.3.3. Cultural diversity 102
    6.3.4. Surf camps. 103
6.4. Conceptual framework 105
    6.4.1. Tourism and social networks 105
    6.4.2. Digital nomadism. 106
6.5. Results and discussions. 108
    6.5.1. Case study: Aloha surf camp 108
    6.5.2. The surf camp 108
    6.5.3. Crisis management: between resilience and innovation 110
    6.5.4. From surfing tourists to nomadic artists. 110
    6.5.5. Perspectives for "Aloha" projects 111
6.6. Conclusion 112
6.7. References 113

Part 3. Business, Education and Covid 115

Chapter 7. Digital Technologies to Support Learning in the University Environment During the Pandemic at UFHB: From Hope to Disillusionment 117
Jean-Jacques Maomra BOGUI

7.1. Introduction. 117
7.2. Digital technologies to support training in the university
environment 119
7.3. Difficulties when appropriating ICTs within academic
institutions in Africa 120
7.4. Improved access to ICTs, the digital divide in secondary education ... 121

7.5. The Covid-19 pandemic as a catalyst for the integration of
ICTs into pedagogy and learning in the university setting 122
7.6. Methodology: meeting the students. 124
7.7. Focus group characteristics 125
7.8. Smartphones, the students' tool of choice 125
7.9. UFHB students' perception of online learning 126
7.10. Pedagogy and experience of online courses 126
7.11. DSIC student critiques of the online training experience 127
7.12. Student suggestions for improving the organization of
online courses 127
7.13. Discussion of the survey results 128
7.14. Conclusion 129
7.15. References. 129

**Chapter 8. The Use of ICT by Students of the University
Ibn Zohr During Covid-19: Uses and Representations.** 133
Abderrahmane AMSIDDER, Samar CHAKHRATI and Semaya EL BOUTOULY

8.1. Introduction. 133
8.2. Contextualization 134
8.3. Objective 134
8.4. Issue 134
8.5. Theoretical framework 135
8.6. Methodology and presentation of the tool 136
  8.6.1. Sample 136
  8.6.2. Questionnaire 136
8.7. Results and discussion 137
  8.7.1. Some results related to the use and representations of
  ICT among students 138
  8.7.2. Interpreting the survey results 142
8.8. Conclusion 142
8.9. References 144

**Chapter 9. Digital Communication for the Continuity of
Socioeconomic Activities in Times of Covid-19 in
Côte d'Ivoire: An Inventory of the Uses of ICTs** 147
Bassémory KONÉ

9.1. Introduction. 147
9.2. Key theories 149
9.3. Method 150

9.4. The deployment of digital communication for socioeconomic
activities 150
   9.4.1. Political-administrative activities in times of Covid-19 151
   9.4.2. Digital technology at the service of companies 152
   9.4.3. Online courses in the education/training sector 153
   9.4.4. Religious services. 155
   9.4.5. Identified obstacles 156
9.5. Recommendations to better adapt digital communication
to managerial approaches 157
   9.5.1. A greater commitment from the state 157
   9.5.2. Greater involvement of civil society. 157
9.6. Conclusion 158
9.7. References 158

List of Authors 161

Index 163

Foreword

This collective work presents varied but convergent perspectives on the methods and means implemented in Morocco, Côte d'Ivoire and Burkina Faso in particular, but also elsewhere in Africa, to limit the disruptive effects of the Covid-19 pandemic on daily life and public productivity on the continent. The authors of the nine chapters that make up the book examine adaptive uses of new information and communication technologies (NICTs) in key areas of community and national life in the countries studied from several angles. These areas include school and university education, the dissemination of information about the pandemic and the sensitization of the population on health and hygiene precautions, the innovative reconfiguration of certain virtual communities, the use of musical and artistic creativity in the fight against the pandemic and the promotion of tourism adapted to the new realities inherent to Covid-19. Also noteworthy is the careful attention devoted to the consequences of misinformation and disinformation that, unfortunately, insidiously infiltrate social media networks daily. This is especially critical as it gets to the heart of the misinterpretation that many individuals and groups across the African continent are thwarting the health services' efforts to raise awareness to curb the pandemic.

Reading through the various methodological approaches used to gather, present and contextualize the data and information conveyed in this collective work, the reader can see the scientific rigor that each author has applied in researching, analyzing and interpreting the data collected not only in the field, but also from relevant didactic sources.

Furthermore, when chapters are profiled in thematic order, the dialectical synergy that links them together becomes evident. It provides the reader-researcher, in particular, but not exclusively, with a more articulate and enriching understanding.

To illustrate the dialectical synergy in question, it is sufficient to take the example of four chapters without losing sight of the intersectionality linking, in one way or another, all nine chapters to each other. The four chapters considered are as follows: "The Use of ICT by Students of the University Ibn Zohr During Covid-19: Uses and Representations" (Chapter 8) led by Samar Chakhrati, "Digital Technologies to Support Learning in the University Environment During the Pandemic at UFHB: From Hope to Disillusionment" (Chapter 7) led by Jean-Jacques Maomra Bogui, "Fake News and Anti-Covid-19 Vaccines: Analysis of Facebook Users in Burkina Faso" (Chapter 3) led by Marcel Bagare and "Ambivalence of the Use of Digital Technologies in Public Communication About the Pandemic in Côte d'Ivoire" (Chapter 2) led by Nanga Désiré Coulibaly.

Chapter 8 presents a comparative study of the use of information and communication technologies by students at this Moroccan university in two academic bodies: the Faculty of Letters and Human Sciences, which have open access to these technologies, and the École Supérieure de l'Éducation et de la Formation d'Agadir, which has regulated access. The authors' declared objective is to verify the effectiveness of the technologies available to students in learning and the forms of use likely to emerge from their active participation in the virtual scholastic space created in response. Chapter 7 offers a study along the same lines, but applied in this case to the Université Félix Houphouët-Boigny in Abidjan (Côte d'Ivoire). It highlights the disillusionment that has resulted from the digitization program for teaching and learning in this institution. In this chapter, the author uses a quantitative research method based on the so-called "focus group" scenario, which allows him to document the infatuation that the idea of introducing virtual learning using platforms such as Zoom, Blackboard and Teams would have generated. He also examines the events that led to the transmutation of this original infatuation into disillusionment among the people and groups targeted in the research.

In addition, Chapters 2 and 3 offer investigations into the abuse of the internet and social media through the spread of false news about Covid-19 and related hygiene and health precautions and vaccines. Bagare and

Coulibaly each start from three converging theses. The first states that the spiraling rise of social media and its ever-increasing influence within all social strata and categories has seriously undermined the informational and communicational monopoly that the mass media used to boast. The second argues that the almost innate receptivity of social media to the ambivalent production and circulation of information, misinformation and disinformation makes users of these media particularly vulnerable to the effects of fake news and conspiracy theories during crises such as the Covid-19 pandemic. Finally, the third thesis elucidates that Covid-19 is the first crisis of this nature and scale to shake the world in the age of social media. Hence, the exponential danger that the abuse of these media poses to millions of users worldwide in general, but in Africa in particular, and most notably, in the case studies conducted by Bagare and Coulibaly, within Burkina Faso and Abidjan. This is all the more problematic because, as Etienne Klein notes, whom Coulibaly has cited aptly, "Our society which is dominated by digital technologies, puts our ability to distinguish what is true from what is false in crisis. And it creates a world where everyone asserts their truth".

Ultimately, this book represents a welcome contribution to deepening and strengthening our critical and objective understanding of the complex confluence between new information and communication technologies (NICTs), and the determination to live an individual and community life in as normal a way as possible during the Covid-19 pandemic.

Mohamed SALIOU CAMARA
November 2022

Introduction

In February 2020, the Covid-19 pandemic became a worldwide health emergency. On April 20, 2020, the International Telecommunication Union (ITU) and the World Health Organization (WHO) created a joint declaration to show their commitment to using information and communication technologies (ICTs) to overcome the pandemic. Despite the restrictions imposed by the pandemic, almost all human activities continued. So that several corporations could survive, these activities had to continue, even if some paused for longer than others. In response, a specific terminology emerged in the public space. Reinventing how we go about our lives has proved critical to remaining resilient in the face of the pandemic. These formulas continued through public discourse and debate during the various waves.

Although the pandemic did not manifest homogeneously and uniformly in all countries, it must be emphasized that the response was globalized under guidance from WHO. At the level of internal health policies in certain states, we have seen discourses that differ from those of the dominant institution. In any case, the crisis has caused the emergence of new technological practices, which until that point had not been used in certain human activities. The crisis has now made them indispensable. We have also seen new practices that positively contribute to the response and could become permanent. Responses to the crisis have varied according to the knowledge as it became available.

Introduction written by Jean-Jacques Maomra BOGUI and Nanga Désiré COULIBALY.

We have gone from rigid restrictions – in the form of lockdowns and curfews – to an increasing easing of restrictions. To a certain extent, technological tools have helped to maintain minimum levels of service in several fields of economic activity. This pandemic spurred dynamic and unprecedented technological innovations. Faced with the unprecedented character of Covid-19, society has naturally put its level of resilience to the test in terms of its ability to adapt and reinvent itself. Social, community and professional life has been significantly tested. Across professions, tools have been used to keep the human and economic activity moving forward so that society could feel the effects of the pandemic less severely.

In the medical sector, technology has made a significant leap forward in consultation practices, prevention, management of certain diseases or pathologies, health information and health statistics. In other words, the technological innovations brought about by the health emergency have instigated new approaches to health: e-health or connected health. For example, digital public health services have undoubtedly emerged in the public sector to help trace the contact cases of those diagnosed with Covid-19. Technological devices developed by governments have also contributed to the response.

In the professional field, the pandemic encouraged the development of telecommuting or remote work. In some, technology has proven to be a real opportunity for evolution and innovation, making us rethink daily work habits and practices. A minimum level of service could be maintained due to a certain pre-disposition of the working population to leverage technology and the devices they used before the pandemic.

In the field of education, teaching had to continue virtually during this crisis. Education systems have put special arrangements in place to provide online courses. Numerous practices have emerged or reappeared to ensure these lessons can run normally. One example of this is the re-emergence of virtual education. Whether in the format of tele-education or television education, the implementation of this practice has occurred with specific nuances per country. Family relationships have also been tested by Covid-19. It became necessary to work from home overnight. The family environment became the place of work, with all the difficulties that this can imply.

This new situation of increased use of technology, spurred on by the pandemic in countries across the world, has been experienced differently from one country to another in Africa.

This book's creators wish to promote international and interdisciplinary collaboration through this initiative, and facilitate the connection between theory and field. In this way, this book addresses all interests in digital technologies and digital communication as tools for resilience during the Covid-19 pandemic in Africa. This book is structured around the following objectives:

– identify technologies, tools or platforms to respond to the pandemic in social and professional contexts;

– identify new uses of technologies that have contributed to the resilience of African populations in response to Covid-19;

– describe the processes through which social relations and economic activities were able to continue in this context of Covid-19 in Africa;

– analyze the uses of technologies throughout the crisis, considering their contribution to the continuation of the activities of design, production and maintenance of structures and infrastructures, but also through the obstacles that these technologies have helped to overcome to help families, communities, private and public enterprises function more effectively;

– analyze approaches and techniques for appropriating or reappropriating technological tools in response to the pandemic in the African context;

– describe the new phenomena of media-information and the practices that have emerged or experienced strong growth in digital technologies in the African pandemic.

This collective work is structured in three main parts. Each part includes three chapters. In the first part, entitled "Covid-19, Information and Communication", the first chapter is "Reinventing Everyday Life in the Covid-19 Era. The Uses of Information and Communication Technologies as Tactics in an Abidjanese "Ordinary Courtyard"". According to the author, Youssouf **Soumahoro**, in 2020, the Covid-19 pandemic significantly impacted the Ivory Coast, specifically an area called Abidjan. According to the study conducted in this chapter, the population seemed to bypass the barriers of daily life and overcome the restrictions by using ICT. These technological tools helped fight against the isolation of individuals socially distanced by Covid-19. They enabled them to communicate with their personal and professional environments, as well as their communities. ICT seemed to stimulate the Abidjanese population to regain sociability while respecting restrictive measures. The role also extended to provide relevant information on the current health situation and maintain education and schooling among students.

Digital technology is presented as a solution to tackle physical limitations, while representing an opportunity for development from an economic perspective. The pandemic has become a lever for the population, materialized here by the inhabitants of an ordinary courtyard, and on the Internet by users who use technology to escape their daily realities, mentally or economically. Thus, ICT is used for a wide range of purposes – whether relational, economic, informational, leisurely or educational. They help the people of Abidjan to build a sense of adaptiveness, as they are tools of resilience, and strengthen social ties.

The second chapter, authored by Nanga Désiré **Coulibaly,** is entitled "Ambivalence of the Use of Digital Technologies in Public Communication About the Pandemic in Côte d'Ivoire". Covid-19 was imposed in Côte d'Ivoire, as in all other countries of the African continent. To inform and mobilize the population to fight against the spread of the virus, the Ivorian government uses digital technologies for its public communication. However, the overabundance of digital tools has led to a potential cyber-dependency, which could harm psychological and physical health. Despite this, ICTs can be positioned as a solution to a real informational need. Indeed, restrictive measures, although broadcast incessantly in traditional media, are not necessarily followed in everyday life. Therefore, digital media attracts an attentive audience and reveals a genuine efficiency on the ground.

Moreover, information is undergoing an epidemic with dramatic consequences on the population, even qualified as "infodemia" by the WHO. Digital communication techniques are certainly efficient due to their quantitative scope, but they are not always qualitative, particularly when the population is confronted with false information about restrictive measures. Each individual is free to express their opinion on issues relating to Covid-19, thus creating a possible cycle of fake news, which can be relayed en masse and start to spin the rumor mill. This situation is a viral phenomenon that is dangerous for the health of Ivorians. The ambivalence of the uses of digital technologies is, therefore, the result of access to digital culture and ICT, as well as the education necessary to untangle true information from false information, considering just how much data circulates online.

The third chapter is written by Marcel **Bagare**, which deals with "Fake News and Anti-Covid-19 Vaccines: Analysis of Facebook Users in Burkina Faso". The author indicates that Africa, which seems to be less affected by Covid-19 than other continents, has witnessed a strong reaction from authorities to keep the pandemic on its territory under control. In this respect, raising public awareness has been a major challenge, particularly through the Internet. The web makes information accessible to any Internet user, which entails a plurality of points of view. In contrast, previously traditional media channels dictated the transmitted information, taking advantage of their monopoly. In this chapter, the topic of the safety and veracity of the anti-Covid-19 vaccine, as discussed on the web in Burkina Faso, is a central component. Fake news is presented as dangerous, especially when it concerns Covid-19, which is, in essence, the first pandemic in the age of digital and social networks. The behavior of those in Burkina on Facebook toward this vaccine is the subject of the article. Many people share conspiracy theories and unfounded information on the platform, where two-thirds of users are uneducated. For others, Facebook is their main source of information, so fake news about the vaccine became accepted by the population, putting their health at risk.

The second part of this book addresses the pandemic as it unfolded in the daily realities of the cultural sector. It is entitled "Covid, Art and Culture". In the first chapter of this part (Chapter 4), Julien **Atchoua** discusses the "Covid-19 Crisis and Musical Creation for Public Awareness in Africa". This chapter tackles the role of musical creation in raising public awareness in Africa. Music (a mix of sounds assembled to form a pleasing whole) is an art form presented as having strong physical and psychological effects on individuals who hear it. Each artist uses notes, lyrics or instruments to share and transmit ideas about everyday life and social practices. In this way, music supports actions that can help to prevent Covid-19. As proof of this, the virus was presented as a foreign disease, especially on social networks. African decision-makers have opted for an informative communication strategy using music.

As an art form, music enables the study of many social aspects inherent to the specificities of melodies, lyrics and internal and external elements. During a crisis like that of Covid-19, the socio-sanitary stakes were revealed. Atchoua presents his methodology and results in his eponymous analysis. The musical works were studied to highlight the trend of health awareness echoing in Africa through the education of populations about restrictive measures and the threats resulting from the virus. However, digitalized misinformation reigns on the continent. Music, which is multilingual and present in homes without any particular social distinction, conveys the preventive message of official national and international institutions in a pacifist manner. Thus, all styles of music and artists represent informative and preventive channels that can help inform a population confronted with Covid-19.

In the second chapter of Part 2 (Chapter 5), Losséni **Fanny** proposes "Rethinking Theatrical Performances in the Covid-19 Era: Strategies and Perspectives". According to the author, since the Covid-19 pandemic, restrictive measures have limited social interactions, including performances in the theatre. Presented by the chapter's author as a source of resilience, the theatre would be essential to individuals' physical and mental development. Several innovations in testing theatrical representations that were already in decline following a prosperous era from the 1970s to the 1990s are being tested in Cote D'Ivoire. Despite certain negative consequences, such as significant economic losses, these trials have visibly positive effects on the potential creativity inherent in situations of crisis.

Constraints induce resilience and resistance. Theatrical performances have used these constraints to develop a creative way to generate renewed interest. Also, the professionals in the sector have been inventive when generating innovative methods and practices that respect the recommended measures, such as digital communication and social networks. Finally, the author of the chapter supports the role of the Ivorian State in the promotion and reinvention of media, culture and the arts, considering funding and consulting many key players working in the sector.

Tourism is a field particularly affected by this crisis. Hanane **Mabrouk** and John **Van Den Plas** wrote Chapter 6, entitled "Tourism and the Pandemic: How to be Resilient and Creative Thanks to NICTs. Case study:

Aloha Surf Camp in Morocco". Indeed, the pandemic linked to Covid-19 has had a detrimental impact on industries worldwide, including the tourism sector, which is expected to be promising in Africa by 2020. Morocco's borders have remained closed, so the tourism sector, the second contributor to the country's GDP, has been restricted to national travelers. However, new ICTs (NICTs) have not been limited by the measures; international targets can still be reached digitally, and there is the potential to reach people physically in the future.

In Morocco, tourism stakeholders have demonstrated the resilience and creativity needed to revitalize their economy in times of health crisis. This article focuses on the study conducted in 2021 at the Aloha Surf Camp resort in Taghazout Bay. There, local tourism workers and their resilience have enabled the development of an innovative ICT strategy. Digital nomads and the well of possibilities made possible by NICTs, including Instagram, have led the manager of Aloha Surf Camp to expand his offer through artistic residencies, studio recordings and a complete package of services related to music, accessible face-to-face, as well as remotely. Thus, NICTs have transformed economic risk from the pandemic and targeting tourism into a force for innovation and, in turn, a competitive advantage.

In the last part of this book on "Business, Education and Covid", Jean-Jacques Maomra **Bogui** analyzes "Digital Technologies to Support Learning in the University Environment During the Pandemic at UFHB: From Hope to Disillusionment" (Chapter 7). In this chapter, he considers that digital technologies, which are now anchored in the educational system in sub-Saharan Africa, would seem to be efficient pedagogical tools. However, the use of ICT needs to be put into context to measure its effects. In the university environment, ICT would be beneficial when it is focused on the student and their studies rather than on the lecture. However, the uptake of ICT in African education is still hampered by operational problems.

While ICT access has grown, secondary education's digital divide persists. The Covid-19 pandemic froze the world in 2019, and social and pedagogical exchanges have undergone rapid digitalization, especially on smartphones, so they can continue to exist. The study conducted with students of the DSIC of UFHB reveals significant difficulties in properly monitoring online learning outside of the physical setting of the school and its infrastructure. Goals for improvement include students' participation in decisions that concern them, ICT training for teachers and students, and support for digitalizing students at university and home. Finally, the Covid-19 crisis was a time of rapid adaptation, a precursor to investing in digital technologies in the educational environment.

Another chapter, entitled "The Use of ICT by Students of the University Ibn Zohr During Covid-19: Uses and Representations" (Chapter 8) is proposed by Abderrahmane **Amsidder**, Samar **Chakhrati** and Semaya **El Boutouly**. Nowadays, digital technologies, also called ICTs, punctuate our daily lives. Always accessible, we no longer separate our professional time from our personal time. Due to the Covid-19 pandemic, universities had to react quickly and adapt to virtual learning for pedagogical continuity, such as the University Ibn Zohr in Agadir. The effectiveness of ICT in learning is evaluated in an open-access institution and one with selective access.

The study shows an uneven distribution of Internet access and ICT use among the student community. The majority have an email address and one or more social networking accounts, with Facebook and WhatsApp leading the way. A smartphone is a major tool in digital access, but its use is hampered by the lack of infrastructure and expensive equipment inaccessible to the average Moroccan student. Also, higher education students are ready to introduce ICT in their pedagogical learning processes, although the digital divide is an important element to consider.

In the last chapter of this book, Bassémory **Koné** analyzes "Digital Communication for the Continuity of Socioeconomic Activities in Times of Covid-19 in Côte d'Ivoire: An Inventory of the Uses of ICTs". The Covid-19 virus has forced all socioeconomic actors to reinvent a way of functioning, in light of the barriers, to maintain their activities. Digital technologies contribute to adapting new managerial approaches to maintain socioeconomic functioning in Côte d'Ivoire. First, digital communication had to be implemented quickly to manage the restrictions linked to Covid-19. This situation has brought to light many obstacles previously buried in the traditional institutionalization of socioeconomic activities. Finally, confronting reality leads to tangible recommendations necessary for a future adaptation of managerial and educational approaches using digital means.

The qualitative study and documentary analysis presented by Koné deal with digital communication, its deployment and its effects in a particular political, social and economic context. ICTs have favored the maintenance of economic exchanges: business activities and the development of exchanges in dematerialized form, including the sale of goods and the provision of services. They have also enabled the maintenance of social exchanges through cultural services. The study points to several areas for improvement, including better government involvement to ensure greater responsiveness, and more intentional involvement of the Ivorian population.

PART 1

Covid-19, Information, and Communication

1

Reinventing Everyday Life in the Covid-19 Era: The Uses of Information and Communication Technologies as Tactics in an Abidjanese "Ordinary Courtyard"

Since March 2020, the daily life of the Ivorian population, mainly those living in Abidjan, has been disrupted by the outbreak of Covid-19. In the context of a pandemic comprising various crises (Saint-Geours 2020, p. 14), a segment of Abidjan residents made up of ordinary people seem to be turning to ICTs as tools to innovate. By following Michel de Certeau's theoretical perspective of the user's activity, this chapter questions the logic that structures the uses of ICTs among these individuals. Using an anthropology of the ordinary (Chauvier 2011) which took, as its typical case, an "ordinary courtyard", it becomes clear that people utilize technologies by adapting them to their projects to reinvent the reality of their daily life. The survey reveals use cases for relational, economic, informational, leisurely and educational purposes.

1.1. Introduction

1.1.1. *Context and positioning of the research problem*

Since the initial outbreak in China and subsequent spread to other countries, the Covid-19 pandemic has not ceased to place what underlies life in society and social interactions into the crisis (Lardellier 2021). With widespread deaths and social, economic and political crises, it continues to

---

Chapter written by Youssouf SOUMAHORO.

disrupt habits and customs (Saint-Geours 2020, p. 14). In Côte d'Ivoire, when the first contamination cases were reported, the State took response measures on March 29 2020 to curb the spread of the disease. It established an exceptional situation by decreeing the isolation of Abidjan and its surroundings from the rest of the country, where the epidemic was concentrated. On the same date, the implementation of a nightly curfew throughout the country was ordered, along with the prohibition of large gatherings, the closure of public places (educational institutions, cafés, restaurants, bars, etc.) and the observance of restrictive measures (regular hand washing, wearing of masks and social distancing in public spaces, etc.). In the same context, by paying particular attention to the daily practices of "people of little means" (Sansot 2009),[1] we have observed that a fringe proportion of the Abidjan population seems to be keeping up with information and communication technologies. An exploratory study on this trend relating to ordinary Abidjanese people allows us to ascertain that we are dealing with an operation that seeks to remedy the unprecedented situation of Covid-19.

Thus, the present piece aims to highlight the opportunities offered by ICTs to Abidjanese people as adaptive solutions to the situation imposed by the Covid-19 pandemic. It is a matter of "uncovering the reasons for acting on the part of individuals by taking into account the diversity of motives and rationalities, and by taking into account the discourse that actors hold about their conduct" (Lallemand 2000, pp. 256–257). The question that this research attempts to answer is stated as follows: how do the uses of ICTs (cell phones, Internet, Bluetooth speakers, etc.) by Abidjanese people contribute to reinventing their daily lives in times of Covid-19?

To answer this research question, we will look at the sociology of uses as inspired by de Certeau (1990). This theoretical perspective puts the focus on the inventive capacities of the user. Users are not satisfied with only consuming cultural goods. They appropriate them by adapting them to their habits and needs to live better in the social order. In reality, "the appropriation of new technologies is a complex activity that gives rise to continuous adjustments between the technique and its social use" (Rieffel 2005, p. 409). Thus, in this work, the concept of use is understood in the

---

[1] The people of little means are the ordinary people, of modest conditions, or in short, the small people (SANSOT 2009, p. 7).

Certalien sense as a set of tactics that can be tricks, tinkerings or "arts of doing" of the ordinary man and user of technologies. This theoretical position leads us to consider the inhabitants of the "ordinary courtyards" as tacticians who use ICTs to circumvent the multiple upheavals in their daily activities caused by Covid-19 and the governmental response measures to tackle said pandemic.

1.1.2. *Field and methods*

This research is empirically based on an anthropology of the ordinary (Chauvier 2011) that places at the center of the analysis "what happens every day and recurs every day, the banal, the ordinary, the obvious, the common, the ordinary, the infra-ordinary, the background noise, the habitual" (Pérec 1989, p. 11). To do this, we are interested in the daily experience of Abidjanese people living in the "ordinary courtyards" in the context of the Covid-19 pandemic. The criteria that led to the choice of this fieldwork are twofold. On the one hand, this type of housing is popular and cosmopolitan, as it usually brings together people of diverse origins, different cultures and modest status (Leimdorfer 1998, p. 60). It is the reflection of the Côte d'Ivoire in miniature. On the other hand, the spatial organization of the "ordinary courtyard" follows that of the village (Manou 1989, p. 310), which implies a communal life where proximity and promiscuity can expose the inhabitants to certain health risks, such as those related to epidemics. This terrain is, therefore, relevant when studying life during the Covid-19 crisis.

We worked on the typical case of one of these habitats in the Abidjan commune of Koumassi, where we live. The investigations occurred at the beginning of the health crisis, between April 4, 2020 and September 11, 2020.

We used the technique of observant participation (Bastien 2007) to analyze how the inhabitants of the ordinary courtyard appropriate digital technologies as adaptive tactics that help the health situation. As residents of the courtyard, we used this status to gather information on the practices of people concerning ICTs. To do this, we used a grid that was intended to be very flexible. Comprehensive interviews were also conducted with residents of the ordinary courtyard in question. In practice, the aim was to give free rein to the viewpoint of "the ordinary person [who] has much to teach us" (Kaufmann 2014, p. 23) about what happens to them. Following Garfinkel

(1967, p. 67), this is to say that the social actors studied are not "cultural idiots". Eleven interviews of an average length of 30 minutes were conducted with the people in the courtyard. The exchanges are focused on the meaning and motivations of their practices and uses of ICTs during drastic measures taken by the government in the fight against the Covid-19 pandemic. The speeches collected were subject to a longitudinal lexico-thematic analysis. The words and expressions used by the participants were then grouped into descriptive categories to give meaning to our research. These words have been integrated into the body of the analysis in italics for illustrative purposes. The names of the interviewees have been suppressed at their request.

1.2. Results

In order to "deal with" the health crisis and its impact on daily life, the individuals in our corpus have deployed several procedures for using info-communication technologies. The following section exposes these procedures as tactics and "schemes of operations and technical manipulations" (Certeau 1990, p. 71).

1.2.1. *Social relational uses*

1.2.1.1. *Staying connected to family*

Technological communication tools were used to break the relational isolation imposed by Covid-19. Indeed, before the decision to isolate the greater Abidjan area came into effect, many residents of the courtyard, overcome with panic and worry, sent their wives and children to the country's interior. In order to remain constantly close to their families, the telephone became a lifeline. They used it to give and receive news. According to the social actors concerned, using a telephone allowed some to reconcile with their wives and children because they were not always available.

> I had never talked so much with my family. My wife confided in me that I had not been as attentive as I was during this time. She told me that the coronavirus kept us apart, but the phone brought us closer.

During the entire period of isolation, the use of cell phones was predominant. Many ICT users admitted that their phone usage had increased more than usual. "When you call a parent, they do not want you to disconnect. They want you to stay on the line for a long time. It reflects a strong desire to see each other again". The digital apps Facebook and WhatsApp were also used for social purposes. As one participant puts it: "these two social networks allowed you to post photos and make video calls. This was more reassuring than a simple phone call".

Another "cunning use case" that we have noted among social actors is their tendency to use ICTs as instruments of community connection. Indeed, unable to meet with members of their communities as they usually did because of the ban on gatherings, individuals resorted to using digital tools. For example, one informant said he created a WhatsApp group to allow meetings to take place as part of his village association. Members living in Abidjan who could not meet in person did so virtually via social media. Our participant adds that he was able to make himself available to the community through the digital interface WhatsApp. He says:

> We have never been mobilized like this. Social networks made people who were never present available when these meetings were held online. This is my case; I could see faces I had lost sight of for a long time. I could spend fruitful moments with my brothers via meetings on WhatsApp while at work.

1.2.1.2. *"Sticking together" to hold on*

The spread of electronic wallets via cell phones has enabled many Abidjanis to access financial services. They can own accounts and carry out financial transactions with their phone chips. What should be private and personal property was associated with the daily practices of solidarity among the users surveyed. Indeed, during the investigations, we witnessed tenants unhesitant to *share* their electronic wallets with their neighbors. This misuse consisted of making payments on behalf of an inhabitant at their request. On this subject, this interviewee is explicit:

> With the curfew, we had no choice but to help each other. Several times, neighbors of neighbors came to me often in a hurry for me to do them a favor so that I could prepay from my mobile money account electricity or channel for them because their accounts were not topped up or simply because they did not have any. They could not go out under curfew to do it

either. Besides, they were sure not to find any workers outside at that hour.

He says the service was not free: "I was reimbursed cash in hand on the spot, with the equivalent amount used for payment. I also agreed to be paid later the next day".

In addition to these cases, acts of generosity between inhabitants of the same courtyard took the form of donations where ICTs could contribute. Some respondents claimed that they often "lent their cell phones for free" to their neighbors to make calls because they did not have communication credits. This form of cell phone use did not begin with the advent of Covid-19, but it increased during this period because "we had to stick together", they said.

In addition, "if a tenant did not return before the curfew time, anyone who had credit would call them spontaneously or at the request of their relative".

1.2.2. *Hedonic and playful uses*

1.2.2.1. *Reconnecting with the pleasures and sensations of everyday life*

Some participants indicated during the survey that, as they were used to going out to nightclubs at night or in *show* and *enjailment* spaces, they were forced to stay at home and respect the nightly curfew put in place by the authorities. This situation created a sense of malaise due to the feeling of seclusion at home. To solve this malaise, they used digital technologies to try to recreate the festive atmosphere they used to experience outside the walls of the "ordinary courtyard" within the entertainment spaces. Our observations highlight that inhabitants would create a *grin*[2] constantly *ambient*, with music played through Bluetooth speakers connected to an Android phone. This technological device was used to create a relaxing and friendly atmosphere.

> Curfew time is like being in prison. At least we have something to enjoy as if we were in a show in a club. At least we do not have to pay to dance as we do in the maquis and nightclub.

---

2 A grin is a space of sociability that gathers individuals around tea. This type of space is mainly found in Mali, Burkina Faso, Côte d'Ivoire, etc.

Figure 1.1. *A loudspeaker connected by Bluetooth to an Android phone at the grin. For a color version of this figure, see www.iste.co.uk/diallo/technologies.zip*

1.2.3. *Emerging from the inactivity brought about by the pandemic*

With the health crisis shutting down companies where people were employed, some social actors found resources through digital technologies that helped them to escape from boredom. One of them speaks of having downloaded numerous video films on his USB key and memory card, which he spent the day watching to "cheat the long time" of inactivity. Another emphasizes how their phone helped in this difficult situation:

> Without a phone, I do not know how I would be able to cope with the unemployment situation. I did everything with my phone to keep myself busy. Sometimes I surfed the net. Sometimes I watched music videos.

In addition, curfew nights were found to be boring for some inhabitants. In order not to go and "count sheep in [their] bedrooms" because they were not used to sleeping so early, some made use of – as the data from the observation shows – digital "ludo" game applications installed on their smartphones. We saw them playing alone or with another inhabitant until they felt sleepy. ICTs appear here as occupations to fill the long and exhausting stretches of free time, which were necessary with the nightly curfew.

1.2.4. *Uses for information retrieval and educational purposes*

1.2.4.1. *Uses for informational needs*

The outbreak of coronavirus caused a great deal of concern among individuals. It was the first time they had experienced such a situation. ICTs became a lifeline for our research subjects, helping them find answers to their questions. In general, it was a routine activity for inhabitants to use the Internet to access information about the disease, which they were eager to share with their peers. This idea is illustrated by the following statement from a social actor: "I usually use the Internet to satisfy my thirst for information about the coronavirus. I consult Facebook and sites with Google to check the *sounds*[3] which circulate concerning the disease". It can be concluded from this statement that the search for information on the Internet was driven by a need to protect themselves from the rumors about Covid-19 and the crisis it created. Similarly, one tenant added that his monthly Internet usage has increased because he is almost obliged to be online all the time:

> I have become somewhat of a reference since I offered up a piece of information that was confirmed on the national TV news. Whenever people in the backyard need real information about the coronavirus, I do everything possible not to be caught out.

1.2.4.2. *Uses for educational purposes*

Respondents perceived these technologies as tools enabling them to educate their children. Some parents provided their children with digital tablets and smartphones, which they learned to use. Also, the children continued their school learning through educational games installed on these

---

3 A *sound* in Ivorian slang, *nouchi*, means information, rumor.

technological tools. In fact, with the schools closing, this way of doing things became very necessary. In an interview, a parent who is an inhabitant told us:

> I did not want my children to be left on their own. My wife and I are not always at home because of work. That is why I bought a tablet where I installed educational games so that under the supervision of their big brother, they could learn while having fun.

We realize that users have assigned digital technologies an "edutainment" role. It is important to emphasize that the children used these digital objects individually and collectively. They were so busy that they spared their parents the fear that they would go and get into trouble. "Everything was like the days when the classes were open; their absence made the courtyard quiet".

Figure 1.2. *Children playing with a digital tablet. For a color version of this figure, see www.iste.co.uk/diallo/technologies.zip*

1.2.4.3. *Uses for economic purposes*

When studying the daily life of the tenants, the researcher quickly realized that the use of technology was, for many of them, a way to ensure the continuity of their economic activities. Indeed, observing and listening to one participant, Covid-19 allowed her to move from a traditional face-to-face business model to an innovative business model based on social-digital networks. As a restaurant owner, she was repeatedly advised to create a page on Facebook to promote her restaurant, but she never did so. Now faced with the State's measure to close restaurants, she found it crucial to get onto social media to keep her business running without breaking the law. When asked about her preference for digital technologies, she said:

> I created a Facebook page and WhatsApp account to continue my business despite the difficulties. I used to prepare food at home. Moreover, people would order the food after knowing the menu on Facebook and WhatsApp. Moreover, we would deliver them to the place they wanted.

Other user's testimonies mention that they created Facebook pages as promotional tools. For example, another interviewee, who saw his business activities slow down, also said that he used his network of friends on web communication platforms to build a new market. This allowed him to distribute many products he could not sell. He explains:

> I did not know that social networks could help me cope with the drop in purchases in my ready-to-wear clothing store. When I posted the pictures of my *zangoli*[4], I got customers. So thanks to my online store on Facebook, I had a new market that was a real help to me in this very gloomy economic context imposed by corona.

1.3. Conclusion

In short, although the outbreak of the Covid-19 pandemic in the Ivorian economic capital was a very painful experience, it meant that using digital technologies by Abidjanites was unavoidable. The study has identified a

---

4 Clothing in *Nouchi*, slang in the Côte d'Ivoire.

range of uses that allowed the users studied to meet specific and pressing material and symbolic needs whose satisfaction was made more difficult by the health context experienced at a time of shortage: a deprivation of freedom, unemployment, the decline in economic activities, reduced face-to-face interactions, among others. We have thus demonstrated relational, economic, educational and leisure use cases that aim to recreate the conditions of life before the advent of the coronavirus disease.

Following these results, we can say that the hypothesis that ICTs were used as tactics by Abidjanese to reinvent their daily lives during the pandemic is pertinent. This is not to say that these uses in a situational context are all new. However, the novelty here lies in their logic of use and the operations of re-semantization and re-enchantment of daily life that underlie them. The uses mentioned above of ICTs were reimagined by the residents of the "ordinary courtyard" studied in response to the paralysis of ordinary activities by Covid-19 and the mass crises that came from it.

Considering the social actors studied, we are dealing with "do-it-yourself" users who show imagination in their use of digital technologies. Indeed, by adopting a bottom-up approach, that is, from the users' point of view, the research has shown the *agency of* the inhabitants of the "ordinary courtyard". The latter have domesticated ICTs by integrating them into their social context and ways of life. This calls into question the thesis of technological determinism promoted by McLuhan (2015), which ignores the power of the user in favor of the technology.

Moreover, our results invite us to put into perspective, in the Ivorian context, the conclusions of research carried out in European countries, which only see the Covid-19 health crisis through the prism of the upheaval of the social order (Lardellier 2021). They lose sight of the capacity of ordinary people to adapt and reinvent. As we have shown, the users studied resort to digital technologies as tools of resilience and reinforcement of social connection.

1.4. References

Bastien, S. (2007). Observation participante ou participation observante ? Usages et justifications de la notion de participation observante en sciences sociales. *Recherches Qualitatives*, 27(1), 127–140.

de Certeau, M. (2011). *L'invention du quotidien. Arts de faire.* Gallimard, Paris.

Chauvier, É. (2011). *Anthropologie de l'ordinaire. Une conversion du regard.* Anacharsis, Toulouse.

Garfinkel, H. (1967). *Studies in Ethnomethodology.* Prentice Hall, New Jersey.

Kaufmann, J.-C. (2014). *L'enquête et ses méthodes. L'entretien compréhensif.* Armand Colin, Paris.

Lallement, M. (2000). "À la recherche des logiques d'action" in Cabin Philippe and Dortier Jean-François. In *La sociologie. Histoire et idées.* Sciences Humaines, Paris.

Lardellier, P. (2021). "Codivisation" des rites et "désordre" de l'interaction. Engagement et pareengagement à l'ère de la distanciation. *Communiquer,* 32 [Online]. Available at: http://journals.openedition.org/communiquer/8344 [Accessed 3 November 2021].

Leimdorfer, F. (1998). La petite restauration en Côte d'Ivoire (les maquis d'Abidjan) : une culture urbaine ? In *Métropoles du Sud au risque de la culture planétaire*, Jean-Paul, D., Émile, L.B., Graciela, S. (eds). Karthala, Paris.

Manou, S. (1989). Éléments pour une histoire de la cour commune en milieu urbain : réflexions sur le cas ivoirien. In *Tropiques. Lieux et liens*, Pinton, F. (ed.). ORSTOM, Paris.

McLuhan, M. (2015). *Pour comprendre les médias.* Le Seuil, Paris.

Pérec, G. (1989). *L'infra-ordinaire.* Le Seuil, Paris.

Rieffel, R. (2005). *Que sont les médias ?* Gallimard, Paris.

Saint-Geours, Y. (2020). Avant-propos : Covid-19 : vers un nouveau monde ? In *Covid 19. Tome 2 : Reconstruire le social, l'humain et l'économique*, Christian, B. (ed.). MA Éditions, Paris.

Sansot, P. (2009). *Les gens de peu.* PUF, Paris.

2

Ambivalence of the Use of Digital Technologies in Public Communication About the Pandemic in Côte d'Ivoire

This chapter aims to describe the ambivalence of the uses of digital technologies in response to Covid-19. Though the use of digital technologies has made it possible to fight back through raising awareness via digital social networks, at the same time, these digital platforms have favored the circulation of rumors and fake news. The ambivalence of use cases is characteristic of the information and digital age in times of crisis. This study was carried out from observations, interviews and documentary research, followed by a survey sent to populations in the district of Abidjan. The thematic analysis method made it possible to account for digital technologies' ambivalent uses during the Côte d'Ivoire pandemic. Two realities are in tension. On the one hand, there is a clear increase in the use of social networks to inform and express ourselves (positive use case), and on the other hand, its channels promote the circulation of rumors and fake news (negative use case).

2.1. Introduction: Ivorian context of digital technology use in the Covid-19 period

This contribution aims to describe the ambivalent use of digital technologies, specifically social media, in response to Covid-19 in Côte d'Ivoire. Indeed, since December 2019, the world has experienced a health crisis that has strongly impacted the socioeconomic environment of many countries. Indeed, since it first appeared in Wuhan, China, the virus has not

---

Chapter written by Nanga Désiré COULIBALY.

stopped spreading. This led to it being declared a global pandemic very quickly. Faced with a new threat, governments worldwide immediately declared a state of emergency and took a series of measures to reduce the speed at which the virus spread. People worldwide have seen their daily lives turned upside down by adopting new measures such as social distancing, mask-wearing and curfews. All resources were mobilized to face this exceptional situation. Thus, technology played an essential role in the response at the international and national levels. Even though the International Telecommunication Union (ITU) considers that the connectivity gap has reduced, currently estimated at 49% (ITU 2020), it is essential to underline that this digital divide has not prevented us from understanding the important role played by digital technologies when it comes to human activities.

The years 2019 and 2020 have been marked by the advent of the pandemic that the World Health Organization (WHO) has named Covid-19. A worldwide response was implemented, and all possible and available resources were mobilized. Governments sought to understand the scope of this health issue, particularly by triggering the alert systems coordinated by the WHO. On Wednesday, March 11, 2020, Côte d'Ivoire recorded its first confirmed case of a person affected by a coronavirus. The Ivorian government has undertaken several actions since the discovery of this first official case of Covid-19. These include the establishment of a crisis committee, awareness and dissemination of preventive measures, the development of an emergency response plan, the systematic detection of suspected cases among travelers from countries affected by the pandemic, quarantine or containment, and management of confirmed cases.

The environment in which this pandemic is emerging is marked by an explosion of communication (Proulx and Breton 2006) and digital technologies (Walter et al. 2019). The advent of this pandemic has imposed the need to take all necessary measures to ensure the correct response. The supply and digital landscape should ensure more effective dissemination of information and awareness-building among the population. Like other countries, Côte d'Ivoire has deployed its response plan, which includes a digital policy. This policy considers the use of technology: promotion of restrictive measures on the Internet, a case detection platform through screening which has gradually gained momentum in processing test results. According to the ITU (2020), e-health refers to the use of digital technologies to support health needs, while telemedicine is the branch of e-health in which telecommunication systems enable the interconnection of remote sites to provide remote access to medical resources and knowledge. The exploitation of the Internet resource should not cause us to lose sight of what Hagège (2015, p. 39) calls cyber addiction in the symptomatic psychological sense: "a euphoric attitude and well-being to surf the Internet, the inability to stop, the need to increase the time one spends on it, a lack of time for family and friends, a feeling of emptiness, depression, and irritability, the propensity to lie, the appearance of problems with a significant drop in performance". Restrictive measures tackling infection rates are repeatedly communicated through public and private media (national and international). However, we can observe limitations in their application: an absence of masks, a lack of confinement of the most fragile populations, a lack of respect for social distancing and an irregular washing of hands. This situation is due, in part, to a lack of knowledge or resistance to the measures dictated, which may stem from several communication factors: the lack of perceived relevance of messages, the inadequacy of certain communication media channels, the inadequacy of interpersonal communication, the large amount of false information and rumors circulating in communities and on social and digital networks, and the health systems shaken by the sheer magnitude of the crisis. This crisis has disrupted daily life by forcing us to reinvent it by adopting new ways of doing things (De Certeau 1990). A new popular culture is being established with this pandemic.

2.1.1. *Literature and defining the Covid-19 problem in the Ivorian context*

It is not insignificant that the WHO and the ITU decided to cooperate from February 2020 onwards. Digital technologies have lent an unprecedented dimension to intellectually driven interventions. For the WTO (2020, p. 1), "the application of social distancing, quarantine and other measures in response to the Covid-19 pandemic has led consumers to make greater use of online shopping, social networking, Internet telephoning, and teleconferencing, and streaming video and film viewing". In addition, the advent of the pandemic has intensified the use of cell phones as a medium for virtual learning for higher education in Côte d'Ivoire (Bogui and Coulibaly 2021). In the 2019–2020 academic year, it was necessary to find ways to continue teaching despite the health crisis and all its restrictions. This situation led to a shift from a basic use of phones for calls, texting and entertainment on digital social networks to a more intense use as a support mechanism for courses or classes.

According to Redouan (2020), the use of these technologies is ubiquitous, and data play a crucial role, whether they are data captured by surveillance cameras, data from Google that allow for the monitoring of certain places or data from telephone operators that allow for an analysis of population movements. Consequently, the use of these digital technologies has become indispensable for monitoring quarantines, analyzing the data provided by telephone operators and monitoring the collective behavior of populations, but also for geolocalization (which consists of locating infected individuals) in addition to digital tracing, which allows for the detection and tracking of individuals who have been in contact with infected individuals. The WTO (2020) has stated that the pandemic has highlighted a critical need to bridge the digital divide, both within and between countries, given the digital economy's central role during the crisis. Many traditional barriers were accentuated and continued to impede the increased participation of small producers, vendors and consumers in developing countries and particularly within less developed countries (LDCs) for e-commerce activities. This observation has highlighted the need for efficient and affordable information and communication technology (ICT) services, such as telecommunication services, computer services and new technologies.

2.1.2. Objectives and research questions

The circulation of information about the pandemic has been as intense on social networks as on traditional media such as television and radio to the point where the WHO (2020) has described the phenomenon as an information epidemic (infodemia). As much as populations have needed to be kept informed about the pandemic, the strong consumption of digital social networks, which is growing rapidly, should naturally contribute to the rise in public awareness. However, in the face of uncertainty and procrastination by public authorities, specialists, and national and international health authorities, citizens and Internet users become or feel vulnerable. We may wish to specify alongside Augier (2016, p. 110) that

> the evolution of technologies related to information systems, the participatory web (Web 2.0), has brought about profound changes in the way of memorizing, processing, transmitting and

receiving information. One of the new facets is the community organization of information sharing and exchange (data, documents). It becomes even more so in the face of contradictory statements[1], controversy and polemics encouraged partly by and on digital social networks. Official information provided by public communication has been strongly discredited. It has become easy for anyone to speak out and produce information.

This observation made the philosopher of science and physicist Etienne Klein (2021) state that, "Our society dominated by digital technologies puts in crisis our capacity to distinguish what is true from what is false. And creates a world where everyone asserts their truth". Vidal (2017) considers that "the uses evolve according to the current injunction to digital innovations in all sectors of activity". What happens to public communication in such circumstances? This study aims to describe the ambivalent uses of digital technologies (particularly digital social networks) in response to Covid-19.

How did the use of digital social networks contribute to the response to Covid-19 in Côte d'Ivoire? Did these tools serve or detract from official public communication during the response to Covid-19? This study proposes a conceptual and theoretical framework that underpins the study and allows us to report the results obtained.

2.2. Conceptualization of the social uses of technology in public communication

Existing works on technological uses outline how digital tools and support mechanisms have proliferated. We are witnessing the digitization of social and professional relationships, and life is increasingly digitalized and digitized. This observation is valid both in the sense of the added value and the loss of value when using technologies in a health crisis like that we have

---

[1] Klein (2021) explaining the cognitive bias studied empirically in 1999 by two American psychologists, David Dunning and Justin Kruger. The Dunning-Kruger effect, also known as the "overconfidence effect", is based on a double paradox: on the one hand, in order to measure one's incompetence, one must be competent. On the other hand, ignorance makes one more confident than having knowledge does. Indeed, it is only by digging into a question, by informing oneself, and investigating it, that one discovers it to be more complex than one would have suspected. One then loses one's self-confidence, only to regain it little by little as one becomes more competent. But from that point forward, one's behaviour is tinged with caution.

witnessed throughout the pandemic. Zemor (1995) defines public communication as a set of messages issued by public authorities and public services that aim to improve civic knowledge, facilitate public action and guarantee political debate. Otherwise, public communication presents the communication operations orchestrated by any organization exercising a public service mission. We can also mention state and supranational institutions, public administrations, local authorities, companies and public establishments.

Faced with a health crisis, the ambivalent character of the uses of digital social networks plunges us into a sociology of uses. Paquienseguy (2005) shows that the various contributions of the sociology of uses have led some researchers to attempt to synthesize this approach. They mainly sought to understand the technical characteristics of ICTs better to distinguish them. Jouët developed this according to two main themes. On the one hand, the level of autonomy acquired through personal and customizable objects. On the other hand, the influence of the digital paradigm in the form of technology's progressive integration into operating modes by its user.

However, the uses of digital technology tend toward recognizing skills in the context of valorizing one's ability to act using digital technology. Recognition within peer networks or a group of established heritage visits would move it away from subordination through negotiations of innovative use cases and expressions of criticism for prescribed uses (Vidal 2017). According to this author, despite criticism, uses of digital technology arouse emotions that have true meaning in the lives of the public, who draw on their prior knowledge to appreciate and discuss them. We borrow the concept of "negotiated renunciation" from Vidal (2017), which is based on field studies that allow us to analyze the ambivalence of digital uses and their meanings. Users are globally willing to innovate and, therefore, to take on prescribed uses.

For Mabi (2021), wherever technologies are deployed, they act as a lever for innovation to different service projects that can be modified and accelerated. This dynamic encourages more active forms of citizenship that change how we inform and express ourselves, debate and interact with our leaders. For convenience, we speak increasingly about "digital democracy" to designate all these practices. However, the realities of the digital world are very varied, and they accompany heterogeneous, contradictory and at the very least ambivalent dynamics. If some of them are a source of citizen emancipation promising to reinforce social links, like the technologies that promote a collective organization, such as collaborative tools for the most vulnerable or the WhatsApp groups of neighbors that have multiplied since the pandemic, others, on the contrary, tend to support more worrying visions of democracy: a democracy of opinions which are not very transparent and instrumentalized, with debates that are increasingly polarized, like the ones that can be found on social networks where fake news proliferate. We collect data using the instruments presented below as part of this study.

2.3. Collection and method for analyzing ambivalent uses of digital social media in the face of Covid-19 in Côte d'Ivoire

This research is both qualitative and quantitative. It was conducted in five communes in the district of Abidjan. Two of these communes are to the south of the city (Marcory, Port-Bouët), two others to the north (Cocody and Yopougon) and the last one is a commune that the metropolis has annexed with a large degree of urbanization (Bingerville). Direct observation was made in the area identified for the research. Public places, such as markets, roads, buses, and places of worship, were used to carry out observations. In the same sense of observation, monitoring digital social networks allowed us to understand the studied phenomenon. Individual (six) and group (five) interviews were conducted in the research area. The people interviewed for the individual interviews were the key actors in implementing the Covid-19 response plan. The group interviews were conducted with a heterogeneous group of people, mostly in public facilities. Two methods of analysis are used in this work. These are the thematic content analysis method and the statistical analysis of data collected during our field surveys.

Content analysis is a research technique for objective, systematic and quantitative description of the manifest and latent types of communication content. The aim is to interpret them (Berelson 1952). It deals with various messages in the media (audiovisual, print, radio), on the Internet and digital social networks (Facebook, Messenger, Twitter, WhatsApp and TikTok). The content analysis also concerns news alerts, awareness campaigns and events related to the 2019 coronavirus crisis. It looks at the content description that involves the container to understand the tools that are mobilized, the reach of the messages and the reaction of those who receive said messages.

Quantitatively, the survey technique is the standard method, considering the unavailability of a sampling frame. However, a breakdown of the population of these different communes, taken from the 2014 RGPH data, allows us to determine the minimum number of individuals to be surveyed. The minimum size necessary to ensure that the sub-sample is representative is obtained via the following calculation.

Municipalities	Population	Percentage	Minimum sample size
Cocody	4,47,005	19.6	185
Bingerville	91,319	4	38
Marcory	2,49,858	11	104
Port-Bouët	4,19,033	18.4	172
Yopougon	10,71,543	47	443
Total	22,78,808	100	942

Table 2.1. *Number of respondents by municipality. Source: Calculations from survey data*

We select a sample of 942 to reduce the margin of error. This sample survey was conducted over 2 months, from April to May 2021. The observational method adopted yielded interesting data. Quantitative and qualitative analysis reveals that digital social networks were, on the one hand, a confidential source of information for the population. On the other hand, they favored the diffusion of rumors. These rumors were also caused by the numerous miscommunications in public communications relating to the pandemic.

2.4. Digital social media, a popular source of information about the pandemic and a source of rumors and miscommunication

2.4.1. *Digital social media, the preferred source of information*

This crisis caused an over-mediation and an over-mediatization of health news worldwide. Dominant mediatization was not only the work of information professionals. Beyond these entertainment functions, the media (television) and digital technologies (digital social media) have occupied the daily lives of Ivorian citizens.

Means of communication	Percentage
Television	77.18
Radio	20.49
Paper newspapers	9.55
Online media	19.00
Digital social networks	49.04
Interpersonal communication	24.31
By relatives	21.66
Religious guide	7.22
Work/school	11.25
Other	1.91

Table 2.2. *Means of communication used for information (%). Source: Calculations from survey data*

The preferred means of communication of Ivorians, precisely Abidjanis, is television (77.18%). Social networks came second with a percentage of 49.04%, followed by interpersonal communication (24.31%), relatives (21.66%) and radio (20.49%). Online media, work/school and newspapers account for 19%, 11.25% and 9.55%, respectively.

By combining social networks and online media, we see more than 60% of the population using digital technologies for information. Thus, in addition to traditional information media (television and radio), people also use digital media. However, it is important to question the judgment of the population on the information that circulates on social networks.

The vast majority of the population (84.50%) believe in the existence of the disease, and 61.46% refute the assertion that Westerners created Covid-19 to kill Africans, against 15.82% who agree with this statement.

In terms of believing rumors, the population seems not to be very susceptible. Indeed, 78.98% of the population think that the disease can be contracted by anyone regardless of age, country of origin and social category. Only 13.80% of the population think that Covid-19 is a virus reducing the world population.

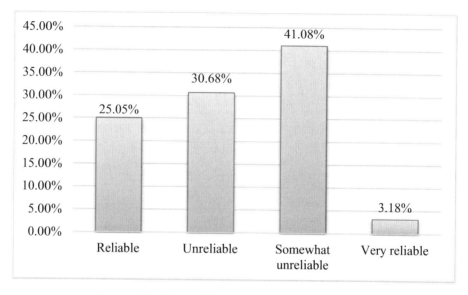

Figure 2.1. *Judging information about Covid-19 from social networks. Source: Survey data, 2021*

Common sources of rumors	Percentage
Television	12.90
Radio	1.81
Paper newspapers	4.58
Online media	10.23
Digital social networks	60.98
Interpersonal communication	34.75
Nearby	26.65
Religious guide	0.43
Work/school	6.82
Other	3.41

Table 2.3. *Frequent sources of rumors (%). Source: Survey data, 2021*

Table 2.3 clearly shows the overwhelming rate of digital social media as a frequent source and medium of rumors among all communication channels used.

	No	Yes	Total
Other	0.11%	0.11%	0.21%
Koranic	1.38%	0.53%	1.91%
Never attended school	6.05%	0.32%	6.37%
Primary level of study	8.28%	3.08%	11.36%
Secondary level of study	22.51%	25.48%	47.98%
Higher education level	12.63%	19.53%	32.17%
Total	50.96%	49.04%	100.00%

Table 2.4. *Use of social networks by education level. Source: Survey data, 2021*

Education level is a key factor in the use of digital social networks. Table 2.4 clearly indicates that users of high school and higher education are the most numerous regarding digital social network use. As spaces of intense media consumption, social networks favor the circulation of rumors about Covid-19. We asked respondents specifically about their opinions regarding certain pieces of information. The graph in Figure 2.2 shows that users of digital social networks have a favorable opinion regarding certain rumors.

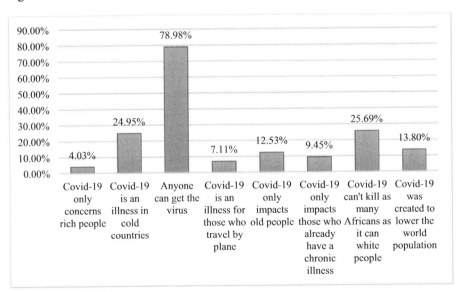

Figure 2.2. *Views on selected rumors about Covid-19. Source: Survey data, 2021*

The population recognizes that the main source of rumors about Covid-19 is digital social networks (60.98%), followed by interpersonal communication (34.75%) and relatives (26.65%). According to the respondents, rumors played a major role in managing the Covid-19 pandemic, and they also believe that digital social networks spread these rumors. Concerning "African solutions" to the Covid-19 pandemic, all focus group participants felt they existed and were enthusiastic about using them.

2.4.2. Rumors and fake news on digital social media, a remedy for miscommunication

While rumors are troublesome in the fight against Covid-19, the typical beliefs of the African population should be noted: belief in God through religious practices (Islam, Christianity and other beliefs specific to African populations) or non-religious practices (intuition, superstition and other practices developed by African populations). The same reactions can be observed among all participants in the group interviews who rely on God as their redeemer. Some perceived the closure of places of worship during the lockdown as blasphemy and a profound disappointment.

Skepticism about the efficacy of vaccines crosses borders, cultural levels, social conditions and many other aspects of human life. For others, especially those influenced by *conspiracy theorists*, vaccines have been designed to reduce African populations. As a result, some governments have resisted offering them to Africa's populations. This widespread distrust of vaccines is reflected in the following excerpts.

> [...] I have two parents who took the vaccine in the West and then fell ill. I was in regular contact with my Aunt, who lives in London, through WhatsApp. But I wanted to do it anyway. So at the entrance of the vaccination center, the guard at the door told me that I was brave to want to have the vaccine. And he added that the guard refused to have the vaccine because some of his relatives got sick after having the vaccine. So all that discouraged me (Respondent from Marcory).

This statement by one of our respondents illustrates the circulation of rumors and fake news by people who cannot inform themselves about the effects of vaccines. Suppose an ordinary person, such as a security guard, moreover from a vaccination center, can dissuade a person eligible for the vaccination from doing it. In that case, it's easy to see the extent of social influences due to rumors and fake news. Thus, in this excerpt, we can see the flow of information that circulates in public places, neighborhoods and on social media.

> We think the disease doesn't exist, so we think the vaccine is useless. For the vaccine to be useful, the disease must exist (Respondent from Yopougon).

These two excerpts clarify the level of people's beliefs and perceptions about the pandemic. The views expressed in these two excerpts are beliefs forged based on a large consumption of fake news on online social media.

2.5. Conclusion: understanding the ambivalence of digital social media use in times of Covid-19

It is undeniable that digital social media use has been influenced by public communication during the Covid-19 crisis in Côte d'Ivoire. The results of this study show that in the face of the sometimes contradictory and worrying flow of information, people had to resort to digital social media to share their opinions on the disease. Faced with public communication that was fraught with uncertainty, social media was the place where people expressed themselves. Rumors were created in a context where sources of information were no longer reliable, or at least did not seem to be.

The question of the cognitive divide regarding ICT use is raised in the context of this study. The notion of the cognitive divide emerged with Kiyindou (2009), who placed it at the heart of the debate on the digital divide. For this author, this cognitive divide goes beyond accessibility or participation in the global network. They propose instructions for use, the meta-information, or in other words, the information that allows us to understand and decode the information. It is a question of seeing and knowing the determinants of the veracity of a given piece of information from the point of view of the user of social media. In other words, this divide goes beyond the possible gap between the individuals who know and those who do not in favor of considering collective perceptions and the value that should be given to these forms of social media. The problem of the digital divide has become, in the Ivorian context, a rather controversial digital bill insofar as the consumption of digital social networks has exploded. In the face of what the WHO has called an infodemia, believing in information from wherever it comes from became extremely influential, making people either optimistic if one was to believe purely and simply in the science or pessimistic when political decisions accentuated paranoia.

The ambivalence we are talking about here can be seen as the result of the problem of access to a digital culture on the one hand and digital social media education specifically on the other hand. The culture in question takes the anthropological dimension of people in their daily practices into account. In the digital domain, culture also designates an ecosystem in which users evolve alongside the "terrestrial" universe, the latter designating material life and its constraints. The two ecosystems are closely linked, as digital communications contribute to structuring, for example, sociabilities (Bosler et al. 2019).

The use of digital social media has strongly influenced social relationships and especially relationships to information and public communication. As a democratic space par excellence, which promotes freedom of expression, social network use appears as a "necessary evil" in managing a health crisis such as this. If freedom is the guiding principle for using digital platforms, we can consider that the expression of these freedoms has been counterproductive in the face of the pandemic. If we exclude the ill intentions of spreading fake news, we must admit that some pieces of content, although false, have influenced the flow of information circulating in the media. A set of factors and prerequisites must be fulfilled, against which the public determines their appropriation or distancing. In this regard, we could share the conception of Atchoua and Coulibaly (2018) when they consider the analysis of Gerstlé (2001). In this analysis of the effects of information, he postulates that informing brings knowledge. However, the effects produced by this action depend on the state of the receiver's prior knowledge and on their information processing practices in the field of experience where it is grasped. In other words, for users of digital social media, it is important to ask about their prior competence in the field before the advent of the pandemic. In this sense, the major factor determining whether information impacts populations is that they must have some experience with information and, more importantly, some ability to give credence to the media that disseminate this information.

Moreover, the Ivorian sociopolitical context has played an important role in the ambivalence of digital media use. This essential factor has strongly contributed to the shift among Ivorians from television consumption to digital social media for information. It comes back to the question of political affiliation. Indeed, some studies have revealed that membership in a political party, whether in power or opposition, determines opinion on the reliability of the information on public service media. Suppose the work of Koné and Zah Bi (2020) has made it possible to understand that political obedience occupies a central place in the relationship to official information. In that case, this variable is a determining factor in the belief in the information circulating on digital social media.

By creating the virtual link, digital technologies have amplified the potential for circulating rumors. This observation is built on miscommunications in media communication at the international and national levels. Goa (2021, p. 126) presents miscommunication as a communicational entropy detrimental to efficient communication. Also, he considers that miscommunication refers to fake news, misinformation, rumors, disinformation, propaganda and the manipulation of opinion in a communicational context. The author adds that miscommunication is a negation of positive communication. The unknown or the unrecognized has favored communication based on uncertainty. In front of the uncertainty public authorities and scientists displayed, a survival instinct has favored a degree of informational speculation, not surrounding the general information media but rather surrounding digital social networks. This observation is especially true since, regarding these traditional forms of information media, the increasingly frightening health statistics were the only information broadcast.

Jouet (2020) rightly analyzes the sociology of digital media by indicating that technologies take part in the upheavals of the technological, economic, political and social order which affect our societies. The uses we make of these technologies must consider a set of practices disseminated in all social spaces, from the private space of the home to the public space of politics. In all fields of activity, we observe a form of mediation of these communication tools. In this sense, the uses of these technologies constitute a laboratory for observing social change. In other words, as much as we can observe positive uses of these media, that is, to inform or socialize, its use can also be negative, as groups aim to create more trouble. Thus, to understand the role played by the mediation of digital technologies in the transformations of our societies, we are required not to confine ourselves to analyzing the uses alone. Other factors, which consider socialization processes, can be considered to access the phenomenon in question. These factors are embedded in a sociocultural, political and economic environment that shapes and distorts them. During the Covid-19 pandemic, humanity has been severely tested. This crisis has shaken many widely held convictions and perceived certainties. Technological innovation and technical prowess pushed forward by artificial intelligence have, rather than being an effective solution, become a factory for a form of artificial resilience.

2.6. References

Acker, J. (2008). Does digital divide or provide? The impact of cell phones on grain markets in Niger. *Bread Working Paper*, 177, 1–60.

Alzoum, G. (2008). Téléphone mobile, Internet et développement : l'Afrique dans la société de l'information ? *Tic & société*, 2(2) [Online]. Available at: http://ticetsociete.revues.org/488 [Accessed January 8, 2023].

Atchoua, N.J. and Coulibaly, N.D. (2018). Communication gouvernementale et santé publique en Côte d'Ivoire : ce que le discours politique veut dire… *Revue de Littérature & d'Esthétique Négro-Africaines*, 3(18), 53–63.

Atchoua, J., Bogui, J.-J., Diallo, S. (2020). *Digital Technologies and African Societies: Challenges and Opportunities*. ISTE Ltd, London and John Wiley & Sons, New York.

Augier, M. (2016). *Pour comprendre la société numérique*. L'Harmattan, Paris.

Bonjawo, J. (2002). *Internet, une chance pour l'Afrique*. Karthala, Paris.

Bosler, S., Pascau, J., Pleau, J., Fastrez, P. (2019). Des concepts au terrain : questionnements relatifs à la culture numérique en éducation aux médias et par les médias. *Communication & Langages*, 201, 41–66.

Breton, P. and Proulx, S. (2002). *L'explosion de la communication. Introduction aux théories et aux pratiques de la communication*. Éditions du Boréal, Montreal/ La Découverte, Paris.

Chéneau-Loquay, A. (2008). Rôle joué par l'économie informelle dans l'appropriation des TIC en milieu urbain en Afrique de l'Ouest. *Netcom/Netsuds*, XXI(3–4)/4.

De Certeau, M. (1990). *L'invention du quotidien. I Art de faire*. Gallimard, Paris.

Donner, J. (2006). The use of mobile phones by microentrepreneurs in Kigali, Rwanda: Changes to social and business networks. *Information Technologies and International Development*, 3(2), 3–19.

Donner, J. and Tellez, C.A. (2008). Mobile banking and economic development: Linking adoption, impact and use. *Asian Journal of Communication*, 18(4), 318–332.

Gerstlé, J. (ed.) (2001). Les effets d'information. Émergence et portée. In *Les effets d'information en politique*. L'Harmattan, Paris.

Hagège, C. (2015). *L'éthique de l'internet face au nouveau monde numérique. Mais qui garde les gardes ?* L'Harmattan, Paris.

ITU (2020). Measuring digital development: Facts and figures 2022 [Online]. Available at: https://www.itu.int/en/ITU-D/Statistics/Pages/facts/default.aspx [Accessed January 8, 2022].

Kiyindou, A. (2009). Réduire la fracture numérique, une question de justice sociale ? *Les Cahiers du numérique*, 5, 11–17.

Klein, E. (2021). Chacun sa vérité. *Été*, 135, 47–51.

Koné, B. and Zah Bi, G.E. (2020). Communication officielle dans la lutte contre la pandémie : effets de l'obédience politique sur les perceptions et croyances des populations. *Actes du colloque, Numérique, dynamiques sociétales et résilience en contexte Covid-19*.

Mabi, C. (2021). "Quel(s) numérique(s) pour la démocratie ?" Institut national de la jeunesse et de l'éducation populaire. *Cahiers de l'action*, 57, 89–100.

OECD (2021). *La transformation numérique à l'heure du Covid-19 : renforcer la résilience et combler les fractures*. Supplément à l'édition 2020 des Perspectives de l'économie numérique, Paris [Online]. Available at: www.oecd.org/digital/digital-economyoutlook-covid.pdf.

OIT (2020). Le Covid-19 et le secteur de l'éducation. Note sectorielle de l'OIT, Organisation International du Travail, Geneva.

OMC (2021). Le commerce électronique, le commerce et la pandémie de Covid-19. Note d'Information No. 1, OMC.

Paquienseguy, F. (2005). La formation des usages a l'ère des TIC numériques. In *Conférence : Enjeux et usages des TIC : aspects sociaux et culturels*, 2, 129–138. Université Bordeaux Montaigne, Bordeaux.

Redouan, N. (2020). Les technologies de surveillance à l'ère de la Covid-19. Policy Center for the New South, Marrakech [Online]. Available at: www.policycenter.ma.

Vidal, G. (2017). Études qualitatives d'usages numériques et approche critique. *Approches Inductives*, 4(2), 160–183.

Walter, J., Douyère, D., Bouillon, J.-C., Olivier-Yaniv, C. (2019). Dynamiques des recherches en Sciences de l'Information et de la Communication. *Conférence permanente des directeurs/trices des unités de recherche en sciences de l'information et de la communication.*

Zemor, P. (1995). *La communication publique*. PUF, Paris.

3

Fake News and Anti-Covid-19 Vaccines: Analysis of Facebook Users in Burkina Faso

The appearance and spread of the 2019 coronavirus disease (Covid-19) worldwide, particularly in Burkina Faso, from the beginning of 2020, has been the subject of extensive media coverage. With its corollary of deaths, this disease has led to adopting health measures to contain its diffusion. Thus, the idea of using the vaccine as the most effective containment measure is constantly challenged by a fake news campaign on online social media, most notably on Facebook. What do we know about this fake news campaign? Why was there so much fake news surrounding anti-Covid-19 vaccines on social networks during this crisis?

In this chapter, we proposed a typology of misinformation about the Covid-19 vaccine to gain insights into fake news around the vaccine and reflect on its impacts on African societies and the country of Burkina Faso.

3.1. Introduction

Like most West African countries, Burkina Faso recorded its first case of Covid-19 at the end of the first week of March 2020. While Covid-19 spread worldwide exponentially with its expected casualties, the African continent remained less impacted. To this day, the continent has not recorded as much loss of human life as other continents, as predicted by some senior officials of the World Health Organization (WHO) (Centre d'études

---

Chapter written by Marcel BAGARE.

stratégiques de l'Afrique 2020). Thus, to preserve the African continent from a health catastrophe, the public authorities have orchestrated aggressive strategies centered on sensitization via the media, considering their influence in society (Idjeraoui-Ravez and Eyries 2015). The Internet has become an important informational media outlet, raising many questions. These are largely motivated by the will to define a better interface between a public space in possible reconfiguration (Miège 2011) and cultural and media industries in the grip of sensitive technological and economic evolutions (Charon 2010). In such a context, the nature of online information, and in particular the diversity of media content offered to Internet users, becomes a central issue. The Internet constitutes an arena where different actors compete to access a media platform. First and foremost, the content offered to Internet users' results from the work realized by the actors who specialize in creating online information. The logic of the media system, which leads to a rather traditional situation of "circular transmittal of information" as popularized by Bourdieu (1996), is made even more complex where the Internet is concerned. Thus, the effect *(or echo chamber)* of digital social media provokes panic, which becomes even more irrational as it is fed by a rarely observed mix of *fake news* and conspiracy theories. In this context, the President of the European Commission, Ursula von der Leyen, proclaimed in a statement on March 31, 2020, that "disinformation can kill". The production of content that promises false remedies for profit is an example of disinformation (Rubise 2012). However, the same content can also be described as misinformation (*defined as false information, but the person disseminating it believes it to be true*)[1] when it is believed to be true and then shared by MSN users to be useful. In the case of Covid-19, responses may vary depending on the varying motivations of those complicit in sharing misinformation and disinformation. However, the impact of misinformation, regardless of intent, is the same. In both cases, people are disempowered, by being actively misinformed, with very serious impacts (Posetti and Bontcheva 2020). This reality is particularly noticeable during periods of conflict or crisis. With the emergence of the Internet, "the comfortable position of the media and journalists as monopolists of information in society is coming to an end" (Remonet 2011, p. 15). The power of journalists and mass media to impose or control debates in the

---

[1] UNESCO, "Journalism, fake news & disinformation: Handbook for journalism education and training". Available at: https://unesdoc.unesco.org/ark:/48223/pf0000265552.

public space is thus undermined in the era of Internet technologies: "The time when they alone had the right to choose and publish information is over. The web strips them of their identity as 'secular priests'" (Bogui and Agbobli 2017). We can thus wonder about the influence of the increasing use of digital social media on the circulation of information in this period of a health crisis. One of the divisive issues today is the use of the Covid-19 vaccine. Vaccines, like any drug, are subject to strict marketing regulations. While the risks associated with a vaccine are rigorously assessed during pre-marketing clinical trials, they continue to be monitored during vaccination campaigns and afterward. Monitoring is essential to assess potential adverse events that may not have been previously identified (Remmel 2021). Suppose all these questions about the administration of the Covid-19 vaccine remain unanswered by health authorities. In that case, the comments of certain personalities in the scientific world relayed by the international media and taken up on social networks do not facilitate the work of public authorities in raising awareness about the vaccine's usefulness. "Are Africans *guinea pigs* for Covid-19?" Two French researchers suggested that a vaccine against Covid-19 should be tested in Africa, which provoked indignation (Petite 2020). This type of controversy adds to doubts about the veracity of the information provided by Internet users about the administration of the vaccine.

According to the Director General at WHO, "fake news spreads faster and easier than this virus, and it is just as dangerous". Covid-19 is the first pandemic to take place in the era of digital social networks. It provides a new illustration of misinformation with dimensions never seen before. This is why, even if it is still too early to draw definitive lessons from this "info-demic", it is important to identify the most critical manifestations to propose a (*strategic*) analysis. From this perspective, this research on the phenomena of the propagation of fake news about the Covid-19 vaccine on digital social networks, particularly Facebook, is being conducted. We will seek to understand how in Burkina Faso, fake news about the Covid-19 vaccine is propagated on digital social media, particularly Facebook. How does fake news influence the level of perception of Facebook users on the usefulness of the vaccine against Covid-19? Moreover, how do Burkinabè Facebook users tend to evaluate the content of anti-Covid-19 fake news? A transversal inventory of all the problems that disseminate fake news will also provide a solution to the various questions raised. Based on quantitative and qualitative analyses, the study will shed light on the phenomenon of fake news on a social network whose use is significant in Burkina Faso.

3.2. Methodology

In this research, we focused on the works published or relayed on the digital social network Facebook since the circulation of the first vaccines worldwide on February 15, 2021. This was the date the WHO authorized the emergency use of two versions of the AstraZeneca/Oxford vaccine against Covid-19, manufactured by the Serum Institute of India and SKBio. Our corpus includes 84 publications related to the different vaccines (advertisements, reports, news articles, etc.) whose content reports fake news. Our analysis method will investigate the texts disseminated (*content analysis*). This is a process "for collecting, describing and processing data" in a reproducible and systematic way (De Bonville 2006). It will be used not only to describe the substance of the messages, but also to analyze the "clear intentions" of the actors through their speech patterns (Mace and Pétry 2000). As far as the perception of Internet users on the issues developed here is concerned, we will resort to the socio-anthropological approach as described by Bouvier, which focuses on distinguishing the scales of observation used in field research, focusing on technical innovations, but also on the reduction of distance between observational methods and the partially experimental interview technique. This will open the way for a new hybrid investigation technique called the observation interview, which will constitute the methodological core of socio-anthropology when looking to understand the subject. In addition to the collection tools mentioned earlier, we have developed a survey that has allowed us to reach a sample of 111 Facebook users, which is fake news.

The research theories mobilized in this reflection are of two genres. The first is of social networks. We look at the works of Dagiral and Martin (2016), which are based on the identification and analysis of new sociabilities and their stakes. They make it possible to determine whether the mutations that come from them bring forward progressive or regressive dynamics. The second was developed by Machiavelli in his work *The Prince*. According to Machiavelli, the simple use of forgery gives particular importance to using secrets, lies and pretenses. He theorizes a pre-modern form of public relations and public opinion management strategies and recommends "perfectly possess the art of simulating and dissimulating" (Darnton 2017). Beyond the purely political use of lies and fake news, the birth of the press will also lead to the similar appearance of a form of proto-press (*digital social networks*), which also appeals to fake news to varying extents (Kikuchi 2017). Far from being a recent phenomenon, fake news and alternative facts are part of an ecosystem of information and the complex relationship between the public sphere and the truth.

3.3. The profiles of Facebook users and their content

Analysis of fake news on the social network Facebook has revealed the presence of four categories of active users. These Facebook pages or accounts that spread false news about vaccines on the social network identify as (1) traditional or digital media recognizable by their identifiers (logos or names); (2) non-personalized accounts displaying pseudonyms or specific acronyms; (3) personalized accounts displaying users' photos and names; and (4) accounts bearing the assumed names of pharmaceutical or medical institutions. Posts from accounts selected for this research must meet the following characteristics: at least 500 "likes" and 1,000 "shares" per post.

Type of users	Number of publications per user	Percentage
Media sources (traditional or digital)	9	10.73
Non-personal accounts	36	40.85
Personal accounts	14	16.66
Accounts with aliases	25	29.76
Total	84	100%

Table 3.1. *Distribution of the corpus according to the accounts of Facebook users. Source: Study on the analysis of fake news on Facebook (Marcel Bagare, February 2021)*

Referring to the values in Table 3.1 and the graph in Figure 3.1, we can see that the vast majority of fake news studied in the case of this research emanates from two main sources on the social network Facebook. These are the non-personalized accounts and the accounts with assumed names or an alias: 40.85% and 29.76% of all the publications studied. The pages of traditional and digital media represent the lowest rate of the whole corpus, that is, 10.73%, and the classic accounts, that is, those which display the name of the users, cover 16.66%. These results reinforce the observation that the development of Web 2.0 and social networks has transformed the circulation of information, traditionally vertical, even pyramidal, into a more horizontal transmission (CEFRIO 2018). Each Internet user can produce content and potentially become a transmitter-receiver of information. Until recently, media professionals (journalists) regulated the diffusion of information, referring to rules and practices that were supposed to guarantee a certain reliability, while also conforming to editorial guidelines. With MSN, everyone can publish, share or even endorse information. It is in this sense that we note the low rate of representativeness of the publications of this type of user (traditional/digital media): some are concerned with their brand image (traditional media) as a priority, they use mechanisms to filter and control the information. In contrast, digital media are often attached to the basic principles of the profession. The media sociologist Bronner (2013) thus evokes a "deregulation of the market of cognitive products". The Internet disrupts how the public informs itself through social networks and provides a convenient forum for any individual or group that wishes to express themselves. However, these new freedoms are accompanied by perverse effects, such as the widespread dissemination of conspiracy theories, particularly fake news on the vaccine administration against Covid-19.

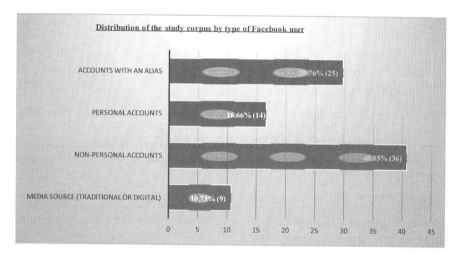

Figure 3.1. *Graphical distribution of publications by user. Source: Study on the analysis of fake news on Facebook (Marcel Bagare, February 2021)*

Referring to the results of the above table and graph and the related analyses, the high rate of users (unidentified and those posting under aliases) who are involved in disseminating fake news on vaccines can be explained by the features offered by social networks. Thus, the so-called "social" digital media outlets have increased opportunities for users to access information, express their opinions and even compete with information professionals (Bougnoux 2014), including during periods of crisis. For Bougnoux (2014), digital social media are seen as great means of mobilization and action, but an important counterweight to traditional mass media in disseminating information. The false "information" discussed here, or fake news, is not similar (see Table 3.2 and Figure 3.2).

Nature of publications on fake news	Number of elements	Number of shares per item
Sound elements (audio clips)	7 = 8.33%	15,456 = 3.44%
Video elements (audio-visual clips)	21 = 25%	252,851 = 56.33%
Written elements (text extracts)	45 = 53.57%	83,678 = 18.63%
Visual elements (images)	9 = 13.1%	96,980 = 21.60%
Total	82 = 100%	448,965 = 100%

Table 3.2. *Nature of the elements of the corpus. Source: Study on the analysis of fake news on Facebook (Marcel Bagare, February 2021)*

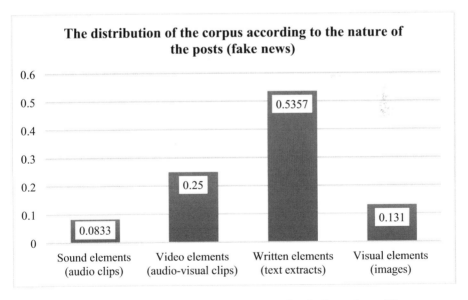

Figure 3.2. *Distribution of the corpus according to the nature of the publications (fake news). Source: Study on the analysis of fake news on Facebook (Marcel Bagare, February 2021)*

Far from being passive, Internet users contribute to spreading fake news. They can even be regarded as the main people responsible for the *snowball* effect in spreading fake news on Facebook and, most probably, on other social media.

Their actions allow false news to spread faster than true information. The results in Table 3.2 and the graph in Figure 3.2 show that the most popularized fake news on the social network Facebook is presented in the form of extracts of texts (journalistic productions), which most often come from media sources and are shared by other users identified in the framework of this research.

The nature of this category of information (text excerpts) represents more than half of the entire corpus of the study at 53.57%. The videos that convey fake news come in the second post regardless of the representativeness of the whole corpus at 25%; in most cases, these videos do not display any precise source, and some come from traditional and digital media.

As for the images and sound elements that we deal with in this research, they are under-represented in the corpus. They cover 13.10% and 8.33% of the total elements studied. Among the reasons that justify the lack of interest of Facebook users in fake audio news, we can deduce this to be in part due to their educational level. Most of the audio elements in the corpus are presented as news reports or speeches by actors presenting themselves as specialists or experts. The level of expression of the actors is such that it is necessary to have a minimum level of education to understand the substance of the message conveyed. We note that out of all the users interviewed, only 39.79% are educated, that is, they have a level of education that will enable them to understand the messages. On the other hand, the graph in Figure 3.3 indicates that 61.21% have no education. Therefore, they may have difficulties understanding the messages being conveyed, hence their lack of interest in or awareness of fake news. This is the opinion of one particular Facebook user:

> [...] What makes Facebook special is its ability to combine image and sound. Like television, we have the chance to watch images, which allows us to use our imaginations to understand the meaning of the images and videos. However, Facebook has become like a radio; we only listen; I think it is not what we are looking for on this channel, we sometimes listen often, but we

get tired easily because they all speak "'big French'" [*elevated French*], this is beyond us, so we pass over it to look for something else. Videos are better than audio... (Excerpt from an interview with MP, a Facebook user).

Another argument we note in this same vein is that of Confucius[2], who states that "a picture is worth a thousand words". This is evidenced by the words of the Facebook user MP, who claimed that videos are better than audio. Confucius thought revolves around education as a source of virtue. In particular, he proclaims three fundamental virtues, one of which is science, which allows doubts to be dispelled.

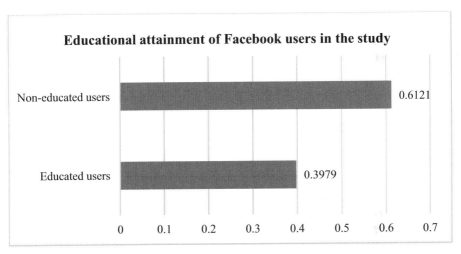

Figure 3.3. *Statistical data on the educational level of Facebook users. Source: Study on the analysis of fake news on Facebook (Marcel Bagare, February 2021)*

Thus, the social network Facebook becomes a kind of panorama or platform for sharing and creating content. This fact is spoken about in the DNA of Web 2.0 (Attias et al. 2010). These social networks provide Web 2.0 features that allow users to edit, index, recommend or archive content, whatever its nature (text, video, audio, images, etc.), by sharing it with all Internet users. The large diffusion of fake news on Facebook, through the "sharing" of content, reflects the reorganization and adaptation of the media

---

2 Confucius, or Kongfuzi in Chinese (c. 551 BC–479 BC) was a Chinese philosopher, founder of Confucianism and one of the most influential thinkers in Chinese history.

system, which therefore poses a problem regarding their responsibility (print media, television, radio, etc.). The *information war* that the media are fighting will generate major disturbances relating to the reliability and credibility of the information itself (Jouet and Rieffetl 2013). On this basis, we can affirm that traditional media channels play the "gatekeeper" role: "They verify, contradict and make sure that the information is reliable" (Mesguich et al. 2012). "They verify, contradict and restore the facts. However, they also sometimes relay fake news and even more frequently, biased or truncated information. It happens even to the biggest titles [...] to be themselves at the root of this fake news" (Michel 2017).

Thus, the notion of "sharing" mentioned earlier is a mechanism for disseminating information on social media and represents, in some ways, the capacity of their users to socially influence others (Mochalova and Nanopoulos 2013). From the work of these authors, we can distinguish two ways of evaluating how fake news and real information are diffused. In the first case, we talk about an information cascade: the mechanism of "sharing" or diffusion occurs when social network users publish their informational signal influenced by those around them, covering the same theme. In other words, we are evaluating a closed world where information can only be acquired within the social network. In the second case, we are talking about crowd behavior. Crowd behavior is observed when social media users post about the same topic in succession, based on both their informational signals and the decisions made by those around them. In other words, we consider an open world where information can be acquired within social media, but also outside (Guille 2015). According to the statistics in Table 3.2, while written texts are in the majority of the corpus, they were shared less by users than the other elements of the corpus.

According to our investigations, videos are the corpus elements that have seen the highest number of "shares" on social networks, particularly Facebook. The "sharing" of videos covers more than half of the whole corpus of the study, with 56.33% against 18.63% for the written elements of the corpus. The audio elements are almost insignificant, as they represent only 3.44%. Thus, the high number of "shares" of videos whose content reports fake news compared to the other elements of the corpus translates to the phenomenon of "viral propagation of information", that is, ideas, products, messages and behaviors spread exactly like viruses (Gladwell 2012). Works on communication practices in the digital age and social networks lead authors to conclude that the speed with which individuals share online content is a vector of contagion (Guadagno et al. 2010). Virality may not be synonymous with popularity, but it is, in any case, strongly linked to it. Moreover, viral videos have gained a disproportionate level of notoriety and audience size due to social transmission comparable to an epidemic (Shamma et al. 2011).

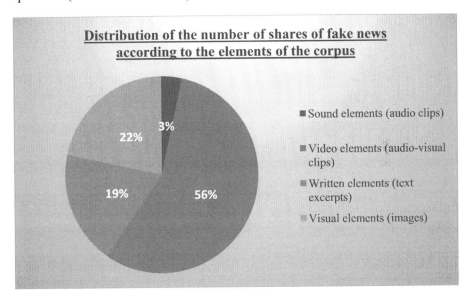

Figure 3.4. *The number of fake news posts on Facebook according to the elements of the corpus. Source: Study on the analysis of fake news on Facebook (Marcel Bagare, February 2021). For a color version of this figure, see www.iste.co.uk/diallo/technologies.zip*

3.4. Fake news in the representation of vaccine risks

The work of major pharmaceutical companies has led to the development of vaccines against Covid-19, giving the world hope for the end of the pandemic (Boseley and Oltermann 2020). However, the existence of these vaccines has raised concerns about how they will be administered and the consequences related to their risks. "While trials have shown that several vaccines against Covid-19 have high efficacy, these vaccines, like all other vaccines, will not be 100% effective", said the WHO on their website[3]. The vaccines approved by the Burkina Faso authorities are the Oxford/

---

3 Available at: https://www.who.int/news-room/feature-stories/detail/vaccine-efficacy-effectiveness-and-protection [Accessed 14 September 2021].

AstraZeneca vaccines, which have an efficacy rate of around 80%, and the Janssen/Johnson & Johnson vaccine, which is effective against severe forms of the disease (less than 70% efficacy for moderate forms).

Thus, arguments about the credibility of vaccines remain at the heart of all communication and advertising strategies initiated by public authorities. These communication strategies would not come without their own difficulties regarding implementation. Vaccination campaigns were to face major challenges, including when it came to managing information (*the reliable type*) in a diverse informational ecosystem, but also regarding the emergence of a new discipline of *infodemiology* and *mesinfodemic* debates (fake news) fed and maintained by the media, including digital social media such as Facebook (Burki 2019). Since the start of the marketing campaign for the first Covid vaccines at the beginning of November 2020, the amount of reliable or unreliable information shared about vaccinations and vaccines increased.

At this stage of the research, it will be a question of analyzing the different themes of fake news about the use of the vaccine, shared particularly on the social network Facebook during this period. Among the themes addressed within fake news information, we will be interested in those related to the alleged effects of the vaccines on the health of populations.

3.4.1. *The Covid-19 vaccine makes women infertile*

This information is purely a construction or can even be put down to a figment of the imagination of some social network users. This fake news indicates that the anti-Covid-19 vaccine would lead to infertility in vaccinated women, who may not be able to produce a placenta in case of pregnancy. According to this theory, the "vaccine causes the immune system to attack syncytin-1, a protein involved in the development of the placenta". This fake news comes from a December 2020 document sent to the European Medicines Agency that lists the uncertainties surrounding the Pfizer/BioNTech vaccine. Agence France Presse (AFP) explains that the text itself specifies that there is no indication of anti-protein "S" antibodies that would also act as anti-Syncytin-1 antibodies. According to specialists interviewed by AFP, it is only a more than improbable assumption.

Fake news about "female infertility" because of the vaccine has a large audience, especially in sub-Saharan Africa. Some politicians and international organizations make a direct link between poverty and population growth, as shown by the work of Paul (1998) in the comparative analysis of four African cases, which are often presented as generally conveying the link between population growth and poverty. This thesis, developed almost three decades ago, has just been reinforced by the current tenant of the Elysée Palace *(the French President)* Emmanuel Macron, who has estimated that the "challenge of Africa is different, it is much deeper, it is civilizational". Moreover, he concludes: "When countries still have seven (7) to eight (8) children per woman, you can decide to spend billions of euros, and you will not stabilize anything" (Blum 2017). Thus, the information that the vaccine could make women infertile justifies one of the conclusions of the World Fertility Survey (WFS), conducted from the end of the 1970s to the beginning of the 1980s (Eloundou-Enyegue and Shannon 1997). The survey found a strong link between population growth and economic development. According to the results of this survey, reducing population growth is supposed to improve a country's economic development prospects and, therefore, its ability to improve the living conditions of its citizens. This belief, although not universally accepted, is based on the reasoning that a decrease in fertility will positively influence the poverty level of the population.

We are not very far from the situation observed at the international level over the last half-century. The proliferation of research on the relationship between demographic and economic growth echoes the unprecedented increase in the population of the countries of the South and the concerns that have resulted from it. Based on models that integrate economic and demographic variables, these discourses have had a large audience regarding the interactions between economics and demography, offering some food for thought on the conjunctural aspect of certain demo-economic theories. Thomas Robert Malthus, an Anglican clergyman, provides a rather bleak picture of the possible improvement of the human condition in his essay on the population principle. Malthus argues that "the multiplying power of the population is infinitely greater than the power of the earth to produce man's sustenance, which is restrained by the difficulty of feeding himself" (Fauve-Chamoux 1984, p. 231). The example given by Malthus of an arithmetical progression of food resources and a geometrical progression of the human species indicates that over a long period, the population cannot grow at this birth rate. Regulatory mechanisms prevent it, and the repressive breaks constituted by wars, famines and other epidemics inevitably occur when the population is too large (Charbit 1998). However, Malthus also mentions the preventive breaks, obviously preferable to the former ones, which consist of people starting a family only when they can maintain it with dignity.

3.4.2. Covid vaccines cause neurodegenerative diseases

Following the fake news about the alleged infertility of vaccinated women, we note another category of fake news that affects the scientific research on the Covid vaccine and its consequences on the users' health. Publications in our corpus report that messenger RNA (mRNA) vaccines cause neurodegenerative diseases. The SARS-Cov-2 coronavirus is a so-called positive RNA virus. When the virus enters a cell, a significant part of the RNA released is immediately translated into proteins because of the ribosomes present in the cell that the virus has just infected. Moreover, according to this category of fake news, the vaccines that the pharmaceutical companies deliver to us would represent a new source of neurodegenerative diseases, or progressive pathologies that affect the brain or, more globally, the nervous system, leading to the death of nerve cells. The best-known and most common are Alzheimer's disease and Parkinson's disease. However, if these diseases are little known to Burkinabé users because of their low prevalence in their country, these likely consequences do not reassure people (users). Thus, according to these publications, an article published in *Microbiology & Infectious Diseases* in January 2021 indexes messenger RNA vaccines, such as the ones from Pfizer/BioNTech and Moderna.

To clarify doubts about this information, AFP reports that the journal from which the information was extracted and published on Facebook is not referenced in the database that lists good quality scientific journals. Secondly, the journal was published by SciVision Publishers, a source not referenced by PubMed.gov, the American database that depends on the medical research agency. Finally, the study is signed by only one author, which is unusual and does not include any visuals. According to the American surgeon Gorski, who committed to debunking false information in medicine, the theory that vaccines cause disease is unfounded. Dr. Angela Rasmussen, a virologist at Georgetown University, also stated in an article in the *Today* newspaper that *the study has no scientific value*[4].

The strong proliferation of this category of fake news about cognitive neurodegenerative diseases on social networks, particularly Facebook, is strongly linked to the social representations of the disease. The notion that raises questions and frightens users is the term "degenerative" to describe these conditions. This notion has obvious negative connotations. These pathologies tend to worsen over time and are, in any case, chronic. The evolution toward a state of dementia is feared because it symbolizes a loss of autonomy and skills, and a deterioration of social life. The risk of chronicity and the repercussions of cognitive impairment seem to give these diseases a frightening dimension. These diseases affect the elderly as well as the young, so we cannot restrict (*stigmatize*) the issue of neurodegenerative diseases to individuals of a certain age. The stigmatization of some patients reduces their access to resources, treatments and opportunities, and leads to low self-esteem, which can affect prevention or care capacities. Socio-anthropologist Goffman has done pioneering work on stigma concerning certain neurodegenerative diseases, physical deformity and deviant behavior. He views stigma as the act of wearing or having worn a stigma. Stigma is an attribute that is considered a source of pollution (Goffman 1979, p. 41). This question thus refers to the construction of normality: by looking at others (*those who are stigmatized*) with a negative judgment, the individual or group confirms its normality, which legitimizes the devaluation of the other.

3.4.3. *Bill Gates and his geo-tagged vaccine against Covid*

This information came from the Instagram account of French artist Juliette Binoche[5], where she shared a video of someone claiming to be a

---

4 Available at: https://ghss.georgetown.edu/people/angela-rasmussen/ [Accessed September 24, 2021].

5 In 2001, she was the most nominated French actress in terms of awards: selected for the Oscars, BAFTAs, Golden Globes, SAG Awards and European Film Awards for *Le Chocolat*, as well as the César Awards for *La Veuve de Saint-Pierre* and the Tony Awards for *Trahisons*. She is the only French actress to have been nominated for three different roles in the same year.

doctor and denouncing violations of medical confidentiality. In the comments, she claimed that the Covid-19 vaccines would be used to put *subcutaneous chips* into the population. This information was widely shared on the Facebook accounts of the users studied in our research. If some Internet users appreciate this denunciation, particularly regarding the danger of the Covid vaccine, which Bill Gates' company Microsoft is said to promote, other Internet users on Facebook accuse Gates of taking advantage of his fame to spread conspiracy messages. The idea that Bill Gates wanted to take advantage of a vaccine against Covid-19 to integrate an RFID chip[6] to control the world's population, particularly the African population, is not new in the conspiracy sphere. It is entirely false information, as revealed by the fake news service of the French audiovisual media "France 2". It manipulates the information about the development of a technology supported by the billionaire's foundation. This technology is used to identify, in countries with poor medical infrastructure, who has already been vaccinated using a patch containing a microneedle, vaccinate people and then leave a mark on the skin. This system does not, however, make it possible to locate the person.

Fake news has origins in recent history, in the work of the big pharmaceutical companies in Africa and certain big economic operators, including Bill Gates. The online newspaper Médiapart titled one of its articles: "In Africa, Bill Gates at the heart of all the rumors" (Carayal 2020). Are Africans destined to be *guinea pigs* for Western scientists? The question is still heating up on the African continent. The low maturity of the economies in African countries and, consequently, the poverty of their citizens would supposedly push pharmaceutical companies to test their products in Africa with no regard for the safety of the patients (Chippaux 2005).

Examples are common on the African continent: in 2005, clinical trials of *Tenofovir*, an antiviral used against AIDS, were stopped in Nigeria because

---

6 RFID stands for *Radio Frequency Identification*. It refers to a method used to store and retrieve data remotely using metal tags, "RFID tags". These tags, which can be stuck on or incorporated into products, react to radio waves and transmit information at a distance. This technology could eventually replace barcodes. But its formidable efficiency poses ethical and confidentiality problems.

of serious ethical breaches. Conducted by the association "Family Health International" on behalf of the American laboratory "Gilead Sciences", these experiments were financed by the American government and the Bill and Melinda Gates Foundation. Although they were also interrupted in Cambodia in August 2004 and Cameroon in February 2005, these experiments continue to this day in Thailand, Botswana, Malawi, Ghana and the United States. In August 2001, similar complications led to the opening of a judicial inquiry. Thirty Nigerian families took the case to a New York court to have the American laboratory Pfizer condemned for testing *Trovan*, an antibiotic to fight meningitis. During this study, carried out in 1996 during a meningitis epidemic, 11 children out of 200 died, and several others suffered serious cerebral or motor sequelae (Deszpot 2020).

> Throughout the South, pharmaceutical companies organize clinical trials in defiance of ethics and patient safety: absence of consent from subjects, summary information, insufficient therapeutic control, little benefit for the patient or the population, etc. Nearly 100,000 clinical trials are conducted each year worldwide, a large proportion of which occur in developing countries, particularly in Africa. (Marks 1999)

The anti-Bill Gates conspiracy theories resonate strongly in Africa. The memory of medical scandals on the continent and the power of social networks amplify conspiracy theories, ultimately presenting Bill Gates as the great orchestrator of the new coronavirus (Le Monde/AFP 2020).

3.5. Facebook users confront the vaccine communication strategy and fake news

Fake news does not only feed populism and mistrust toward science. It also has serious consequences on all sectors of activity, including public health. Fake news can be used as a tool for manipulation or propaganda, which is why we can understand the assertion that "a lie repeated ten times remains a lie; repeated ten thousand times, it becomes a truth" (Rubise 2012). Fake news has always existed, but the phenomenon seems to have increased due to the virality of information circulation enabled by the digital revolution. Let us consider the anti-Covid vaccination campaigns (a result of the communication crisis) as the response used to mitigate the harmful consequences of this health crisis (in order to accompany the measures applied, or restore confidence in the reputation or the capacity of the public authorities to manage the crisis). This one is thus carried out reactively and not proactively (De Mazenod and Huyghe 2010). The survey was carried out among the various users of the social network Facebook whose accounts are the subject of this analysis. Many other users show results somewhat similar to the positions taken by the authors mentioned above. The graph below conveys the trends surrounding the level of use to be vaccinated or not among the latter group. Although the surveys were sent to more than 100 users, only two agreed to be questioned during surveys. Questions were about the user's opinion on the vaccine. The results are shown in the graph in Figure 3.5.

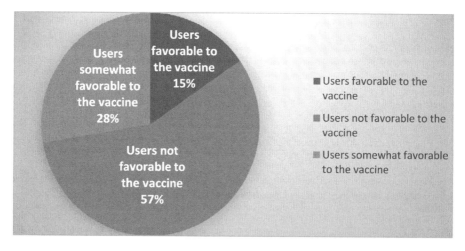

Figure 3.5. *Trends in Facebook users' choices of vaccines. Source: Study on the analysis of fake news on Facebook (Marcel Bagare, February 2021). For a color version of this figure, see www.iste.co.uk/diallo/technologies.zip*

The data that show the number of users who refuse vaccines cover about 57% of the overall opinions of the study. On the other hand, a minority of users have a favorable opinion, that is, 15% of the total opinions of the respondents. Note that 28% of users remain skeptical about the vaccine.

It should be noted that fake news influences a good part of the users of the social network Facebook. The accumulation of contradictory information from fake news ends up being at the origin of the behavior of the masses, as it encourages people to refuse the vaccine, as attested by the words of this Internet user:

> It is impossible to break away from social networks, especially in these times of pandemic when news is coming from everywhere on Covid-19. Facebook is our first source of information because it is the users themselves who are spreading the news. The information that reaches us other than that of the government authorities on the vaccine is not at all reassuring. According to our sources, there is more danger in getting vaccinated. My reluctance to get vaccinated against Covid was born from social networks. (Excerpt from an interview with PM, a Facebook user).

Fake news largely affects a user's choice of vaccine. Some people, in this case, the skeptics, rely on often erroneous information about the origin of the vaccine to assert that it is unsafe and evokes alleged side effects. The controversy maintained by official media channels and shared on social networks about the occurrence of about 30 cases of post-vaccination bleeding disorders in Europe after the administration of the British/Swedish vaccine "AstraZeneca" (Lecrubier 2021) has not helped to improve the messages being transmitted about the vaccination campaigns in Burkina Faso. Indeed, this vaccine was the first to be made available to Burkinabé users. The reluctance of Internet users to use the vaccine is based on this information, although accredited organizations have corrected it. Professor Tim Spector of King's College London (KCL), who led the study based on data from the vaccine research application, said: "Vaccines still offer high levels of protection for the majority of the population, particularly against the Delta variant, so we still need as many people as possible to be fully immunized". This correction on the doubts surrounding the AstraZeneca vaccine did not positively influence the user's choice.

> As long as the AstraZeneca vaccine is involved, I will never be vaccinated because the consequences are serious and many African countries have refused this vaccine. The media reports that European countries have refused stocks of the *AstraZeneca* vaccine... In any case, this vaccine will not come through me,

and if the American vaccines arrive, I will go for it because the Americans do not make just anything [...]. (Excerpt from an interview with O.R., an Internet user on Facebook).

To this end, the sociologist Dominique Cardon, known for his work on the Internet, believes that we should not give in to panic. Rather, we should relativize on the basis that there is a form of technological determinism: it is indeed true that the side effects of all technological innovations are overestimated. The author, therefore, invites us to look at the scales of visibility: very few accounts on social networks have a high visibility (*measured in millions of "followers"*), and most fake news or conspiracy theories circulate in micro-niches, what he calls the *caves of the Net* (Cardon 2020). Fake news only comes out when it is picked up by large media or Internet users with very high visibility. It is closely correlated to the state of society and its media ecosystem. Moreover, Cardon cites studies that have also shown that the people who saw the fake news that flourished during the presidential elections in the United States are people who were exposed to it. That is to say that *those exposed to fake news are already convened militants*. This is called the "selective exposure phenomenon" (Cardon 2019). Thus, it would be presumptuous to make social networks alone the ideal culprit and to think that the technological tool, on its own, produces the effects that we attribute to it. This does not mean that there are no problems or risks, but they should be measured and analyzed seriously.

3.6. Conclusion

The rise of digital media or social media has helped to reduce the power of the mass media over the control and flow of information and, at the same time, the power of the government to exert control over them. However, these new media are not immune to misinformation and can, like the mass media, become formidable means of propaganda. Within this framework, we have questioned the stakes of the informational dynamics on social networks, notably fake news, around the Covid vaccine. Beyond the conjunctural explanations linked to the exceptional character of the Covid-19 epidemic, the accompanying infodemia (fake news) confirms that the destabilizing effects of digital social networks have become substantial in light of the current crises. This has reached a point at which, from now on and for a long time to come, there will be structural issues for (*public health*) security. Therefore, the circulation of fake news directly affects the functioning of the public sphere in general, especially during anti-Covid vaccination campaigns, which constitute important moments for propaganda actions. However, as researchers MacKinnon (2012) and Boyd (2017) have stated, what is truly at stake when it comes to the circulation of these contents is a will to control informational ecosystems, particularly on socio-numerical networks.

Analyzing the Facebook accounts of our corpus that have seen the virality of the most important fake news pieces ultimately allows us to highlight several interesting features. Fake news is mostly conveyed through audio-visual media (*videos*) whose contents express concern about women's health (fertility) or neurodegenerative diseases, examples of sensitive health topics, especially on the African continent. They are based on information that has not been cross-checked or qualified as false by the specialized bodies, making corrections using the specific codes of social networks. However, these pieces of information receive a low level of engagement compared to accounts that are likely to spread fake news. While this study focused on studying the virality of fake news on social networks, the context of its publication is a strong reminder that social networks are likely to facilitate the sharing of other forms of harmful content, such as those calling for or encouraging health incivism: the refusal to be vaccinated. Understanding how different forms of content spread on platforms will therefore remain a central issue in times of health crisis related to Covid-19.

3.7. References

Attias, C., Brayer, C., Salvatore, B., Jacquot, C., Strul, R. (2010). Les médias sociaux. *IAB France*, 5–34 [Online]. Available at: https://www.iabfrance.com/sites/www.iabfrance.com/files/atoms/files/les-medias-sociaux-def-a5.pdf [Accessed 8 January 2023].

Blum, E. (2017). Après les déclarations de Macron sur la natalité en Afrique, que disent les chiffres ? *Le Monde* [Online]. Available at: https://www.lemonde.fr/afrique/article/2017/07/12/apres-les-declarations-de-macron-sur-la-natalite-en-afrique-la-verite-des-chiffres_5159751_3212.html [Accessed 14 September 2021].

Bogui, J.-J. and Agbobli, C. (2017). L'information en périodes de conflits ou de crises : des médias de masse aux médias sociaux numériques. *Communication, technologies et développement*, 4, 1–14.

Boseley, S. and Oltermann, P. (2020). Covid-19 vaccine candidate is 90% effective, says the manufacturer. *The Guardian* [Online]. Available at: https://www.theguardian.com/world/2020/nov/09/covid-19-vaccine-candidate-effective-pfizer-biontech [Accessed 14 September 2021].

Bougnoux, D. (2014). Médias et démocratie. La fonction des médias dans la démocratie. *Cahiers français* (La Documentation française) [Online]. Available at: http://www.ladocumentationfrancaise.fr/var/storage/libris/3303330403389/3303330403389_EX.pdf [Accessed 6 September 2021].

Bourdieu, P. (1996). *The Rules of Art: Genesis and Structure of the Literary Field.* Stanford University Press, Stanford, CA.

Boyd, D. (2017). The information war has begun. *Apophenia* [Online]. Available at: https://www.zephoria.org/thoughts/archives/2017/01/27/the-information-war-has-begun.html [Accessed 29 September 2021].

Bronner, G. (2013). *La démocratie des crédules.* PUF, Paris.

Burki, T. (2019). Vaccine misinformation and social media. *The Lancet Digital Health* [Online]. Available at: https://doi.org/10.1016/S2589-7500(19)30136-0.

Carayal, R. (2020). En Afrique, Bill Gates au cœur de toutes les rumeurs. *Médiapart* [Online]. Available at: https://www.mediapart.fr/journal/international/160420/en-afrique-bill-gates-au-coeur-de-toutes-les-rumeurs?onglet=full [Accessed 27 September 2021].

Cardon, D. (2019). Pourquoi avons-nous si peur des fake news ? *AOC*, 2/2 [Online]. Available at: https://aoc.media/analyse/2019/06/21/pourquoi-avons-nous-si-peur-des-fake-news-2-2/ [Accessed 29 September 2021].

Cardon, D. (2020). Culture numerique. *Open Edition Journals: Communication* [Online]. Available at: https://journals.openedition.org/communication/11826 [Accessed 29 September 2021].

CE Commission Européenne (2018). A multi-dimensional approach to disinformation. Report of the independent High-level Group on fake news and online disinformation. Publications Office of the European Union, Luxembourg.

CEFRIO (2018). Les médias sociaux au Québec. *NETendances* [Online]. Available at: https://cefrio.qc.ca/media/2023/netendances-2018_medias-sociaux.pdf [Accessed 3 September 2021].

Centre d'études stratégiques de l'Afrique (2020). Cartographie des facteurs de risque de propagation du Covid-19 en Afrique. *Eclairage*, 1–14 [Online]. Available at: https://africacenter.org/spotlight/mapping-risk-factors-spread-covid-19-africa/ [Accessed 8 January 2023].

Charbit, Y. (1998). Malthus populationniste ? Une lecture transdisciplinaire. *Population*, 113–137.

Chippaux, J. (2005). L'Afrique, cobaye de Big Pharma. *Le Monde Diplomatique* [Online]. Available at: https://www.monde-diplomatique.fr/2005/06/CHIPPAUX/12513 [Accessed 27 September 2021].

Darnton, R. (2017). La longue histoire des "fake news". *Le Monde* [Online]. Available at: https://www.lemonde.fr/idees/article/2017/02/20/la-longue-histoire-des-fake-news_5082215_3232.html [Accessed 1 September 2021].

De Bonville, J. (2006). *L'analyse de contenu des médias.* De Boeck, Brussels.

De Mazenod, X. and Huyghe, F.-B. (2010). *Influence et réputation sur Internet à destination de manager – A l'usage des managers désemparés.* SAS Adverbe, Paris.

Deszpot, T. (2020). Un vaccin financé par Bill Gates à l'origine d'une épidémie de polio en Afrique ? Des accusations fallacieuses. *LCI* [Online]. Available at: https://www.lci.fr//sante/un-vaccin-finance-par-bill-gates-a-l-origine-d-une-epidemie-de-polio-en-afrique-des-accusations-fallacieuses-2164225.html [Accessed 27 September 2021].

Elounda-Enyegue, P. and Shannon, S.C. (1997). Davis & Blake and Becker in discrete time: From verbal to quantitative theories of fertility demand. *Annual Meeting of the Population Association of America*, 306–332.

Fauve-Chamoux. A. (1984). *Malthus hier et aujourd'hui.* Éditions du CNRS, Paris.

Gladwell, M. (2012). *Le point de bascule : comment faire une grande différence avec de très petites choses.* Flammarion, Paris.

Goffman, E. (1979). *Études sur la condition sociale des malades mentaux et autres reclus.* Les Éditions de Minuit, Paris.

Guadagno, R., Cialdini, R., Evron, G. (2010). What about Estonia? A social psychological analysis of the first Internet war. *CyberPsychology, Behavior, and Social Networking*, 447–453.

Guille, A. (2015). Diffusion de l'information dans les médias sociaux : modélisation et analyse. *HAL (Archives Ouvertes)*, 1–190.

Idjeraoui-Ravez, L. and Eyries, A. (2015). Grégory DERVILLE (2013), Le pouvoir des médias. *Communication*, 33(1) [Online]. Available at: http://communication.revues.org/5319 [Accessed 30 August 2021].

Jouet, J. and Rieffetl, R. (2013). *S'informer à l'ère numérique.* Presse Universitaire de Rennes, Rennes.

Kikuchi, C. (2017). Vu du Moyen Âge : Philippe le Bel, un amateur de fake news. *The Conversation* [Online]. Available at: https://theconversation.com/vu-du-moyen-age-philippe-le-bel-un-amateur-de-fake-news-79541 [Accessed 1 September 2021].

Le Monde/AFP (2020). Les thèses conspirationnistes anti-Bill Gates résonnent puissamment en Afrique. *Le Monde* [Online]. Available at: https://www.lemonde.fr//afrique/article/2020/05/29/les-theses-conspirationnistes-anti-bill-gates-resonnent-puissamment-en-afrique_6041172_3212.html [Accessed 27 September 2020].

Lecrubier, A. (2021). Thromboses et vaccin AstraZeneca : 30 cas douteux sur 5 millions d'européens vaccinés. *Medscape* [Online]. Available at: https://francais.medscape.com//voirarticle/3606973 [Accessed 29 September 2021].

Mace, G. and Pétry, F. (2000). *Guide d'élaboration d'un projet de recherche*, 2nd edition. Presses de l'Université Laval, Quebec.

MacKinnon, R. (2012). *Consent of the Networked. The Worldwide Struggle for Internet Freedom.* Basic Books, New York.

Marks, H. (1999). La médecine des preuves : histoire et anthropologie des essais cliniques (1900-1990). Institut Synthélabo pour le progrès de la connaissance, Paris.

Martin, O. and Dagiral, É. (eds) (2016). *L'ordinaire d'internet. Le web dans nos pratiques et relations sociales*. Armand Colin, Paris.

Matteo, M. (2020). Covid-19 : médias et réseaux sociaux africains mettent en cause un virus venu d'ailleurs. *Le Monde*, 11–12.

Mesguich, V., Pierre, J., Alloing, C., Gallezot, G., Serres, A., Peirano, R., Martinet, F. (2012). Enjeux et dimensions. *Documentaliste-Sciences de l'Information*, 49(1), 24–45.

Michel, P. (2017). "Post-vérité" et "fake news" : fausses clartés et points aveugles. *Acrimed.org* [Online]. Available at: http:www.acrimed.org/Post-verite-et-fake-news-fausses-clartes-et [Accessed 7 September 2021].

Miège, B. (2011). Theorizing the cultural industries: Persistent specificities and reconsiderations. *The Handbook of Political Economy of Communications*, 83–108.

Mochalova, A. and Nanopoulos, A. (2013). On the role of centrality in information diffusion in social networks. *ECIS 2013 Completed Research*, 101 [Online]. Available at: https://aisel.aisnet.org/ecis2013_cr/101.

Paul, M. (1998). Population, pauvreté et dégradation de l'environnement en Afrique : fatale attraction ou liaisons hasardeuses ? *Natures–Sciences–Sociétés*, 6, 27–34.

Petite, S. (2020). Les Africains "cobayes" contre le Covid-19 ? Le grand malentendu. *Le Temps* [Online]. Available at: https://www.letemps.ch/monde/africains-cobayes-contre-covid19-grand-malentendu [Accessed 30 August 2021].

Posetti, J. and Bontcheva, K. (2020). Désinfodémie : déchiffrer la désinformation sur le Covid-19. *UNESCO*, 1–18.

Ramonet, I. (2011). *L'Explosion du journalisme. Des médias de masse à la masse de médias*. Éditions Galilée, Paris.

Remmel, A. (2021). Why is it so hard to investigate the rare side effects of Covid vaccines? *Nature*, 38–53.

Rubise, P. (2012). *Manipulations, rumeurs, désinformations, des sociétés en danger*. L'Harmattan, Paris.

Shamma, D.A., Yew, J., Kennedy, L., Churchill, E.F. (2011). Viral actions: Predicting video view counts using synchronous sharing behaviors. *Association for the Advancement of Artificial Intelligence*.

PART 2

Covid, Art and Culture

4

Covid-19 Crisis and Musical Creation for Public Awareness in Africa

To sensitize populations, specifically African ones, against the threats that Coronavirus presents to the world and the continent, several types of social actors became mobilized, including musical artists who created works of artistic value performed in public spaces. Indeed, the creation of music constituted an integral part of the communication channels during the crisis, deployed as part of a health prevention strategy against this contemporary issue.

Raising public awareness against Covid-19 was thus an opportunity for African musicians to participate in the fight against the pandemic through their works. In Africa, musicians have undoubtedly contributed to awareness campaigns aimed at populations in various local and official languages, using audible tones. Nevertheless, given the widespread propagation of prevention communication, but also of denunciation and production of fake news via digital social networks, it seemed important to us to take stock of these artistic works to explore the motivations and forms of commitment from African artists in this fight against the pandemic in question.

4.1. Introduction: musical creation for prevention

4.1.1. *Music as a support mechanism and collective commitment*

Through critical lyrics, rhythm, melody and the varying degrees of emotion it evokes, music produces diverse effects on its audience of individuals. Music is perceived as an art form that pleasingly combines

---

Chapter written by Julien ATCHOUA.

sounds. Music transmits information through speech, song, sounds and instruments in its constructed form and when translated into a communication object. It shows a commitment of the artist to transmit their vision of society. It is a medium that makes comments on practices of daily life and social practices (Kolé and Adou 2019). It is based on mental construction that allows us to understand how reality is played out. This reality is reproduced by an artist who stages it for the benefit of their consumer audience through the mechanism of reconstruction, characteristic of the classic work of art. At this level, the communication of information is, according to Muchielli (2001) when referring to Quéré, a shared activity that, when it progresses, can construct common meanings which serve as reference points for human exchanges. Music appears then in the fight against the Coronavirus pandemic in the world and Africa as an element that can trigger specific behaviors and can thus plays an important part in disease prevention. Music can therefore constitute a means to accompany or criticize how governing bodies are dealing with the Covid-19 crisis.

In this sense, the importance of musical work as a communication channel in the sensitization against the epidemiological risks linked to Covid-19 seems plausible. It constitutes, without a doubt, a form of displaying commitment by African musical artists. In other words, music appears to be a powerful support mechanism for disseminating information to target audiences in the international and local context of a frantic search to save the world from the Coronavirus disease. It is essential to awaken consciences, specifically in the face of a set of behaviors that risk propagating the Covid-19 virus across world populations and in Africa in particular.

4.1.2. *Covid-19, a reality in Africa*

Covid-19 is generally perceived by African populations as a "disease created by others", even "of the whites" or even "of the big guys", as attested by numerous pieces of fake news that have circulated on digital social networks. The spread of the disease in this continent has falsely shown all theories and information about an unscathed Africa. Covid-19 has taken hold on the black continent. Subject to various forms of interpretation which range from the creation of rumors to the supposed facts that have spread among urban and rural communities, Coronavirus has caused African elites to mobilize, specifically governments that have made this fight one of the priorities when thinking about how to manage their power. From individual decisions to concerted actions through pan-African organizations such as the African Union's (AU) Center for Disease Control and Prevention (CDC), the West African Health Organization (WAHO) and the African Development Bank (AfDB), African decision-makers have used their voices to slow the progression of Covid-19, which is, of course, a health threat, but which also has economic and social implications. The pandemic could cause negative economic growth levels of –0.8% and –1.1% instead of the +3.4 initially forecasted by the World Bank. This economic downturn constitutes a threat of losing about 20 million jobs on the continent (Le Point d'Afrique 2020).

In the face of all the statistics that predicted the worst possible situation in Africa, African elites and their supporters reacted by starting joint actions and communication strategies so that "the Coronavirus would quickly become a distant memory" (Backman 2020). On April 23, 2020, a videoconference conducted at the West African Heads of State at the Economic Community of West African States Extraordinary Summit (ECOWAS) set out to discuss modalities for combating Covid-19. This meeting resulted in joint commitments, pointing to the reactions of African leaders to join efforts and eradicate the pandemic from their territories.

However, implementing restrictive measures that impact the greatest number of citizens of the continent remains a communicational enigma, specifically in the face of traditional beliefs, rumors and other fake news for which digital social networks are the main means of promotion. The need to understand that "[...] the great speeches in 'big French', as they say in West Africa, or the managerial declarations of some English-speaking leaders, must be translated into the languages spoken in the streets and countryside of Africa" (RFI 2020).

For communication strategies that aim to increase the adoption of anti-Covid-19 behaviors in Africa, musical creation appears to complement the awareness-raising activities set forward by populations.

All the measures designed to act against Covid-19 have not left the international music world indifferent, and African artists, in particular, have been involved at various levels. In a way, African music has imbued communication around Covid-19 with messages containing largely preventive content. But these are not insignificant artistic commitments. Following the example of Jean Jacques Goldman, who uses the phrase "they save lives" to pay tribute to caregivers in Europe, Koffi Olomidé has produced the "Coronavirus assassin", the Senegalese rap collective called "y en a marre" created "Fagaru ci corona" (prevent the Coronavirus in Wolof), and so musical artists have raised their voices against the Coronavirus pandemic.

4.1.3. *The fundamental questions*

This study focuses on these aspects and forms of artistic engagement from those who produce musicalized information in the fight against Covid-19. The question is then to evaluate how preventive measures against the disease are translated into African musical works. What do the songs created by African artists convey in this respect? What kind of social commitment do their productions reflect? The answer to such concerns requires us to analyze the content of a corpus of 10 musical works using the enunciative and argumentative analysis methods recommended by Charaudeau (2014). They allow us to identify the meaning of the messages conveyed through the musical works created and the artistic motivations behind them. This analysis finds its foundation in the constructivist theory thought about by Quéré (cited by Mucchielli 2001, p. 112) as "a mutual shaping of a common world using conjugated action". The contribution of these sonic messages conceived in the context of health prevention remains sensitive; they can be regarded when it comes to crisis communication and how it is perceived as it is constructed in African musical works. In other words, like any other context, the health environment currently being experienced worldwide could allow us to show that some musical artists, thanks to their leadership, compose sonic messages that denounce the excesses of decision-makers and the defects of society through their works. In some other cases, constructing musical discourse implies transmitting the information.

This exploratory study allows us to justify such assumptions through the methodological approach presented below.

4.2. Musical information and the Covid-19 crisis in Africa: collecting and deciphering content

4.2.1. *Objective of the approach*

To be interested in an artistic production or piece of content is to study many social representations that emerge from it. It also means revealing the socio-sanitary realities of a population in crisis. Here, it is a question of relying on a set of concepts from the African artistic sphere that reveal modes of constructing reality and discourses for musical communication. These discourses appear in specific forms when transferring health information via melodies during this crisis. Drawing a parallel between this theoretical position and the health crisis experienced in Africa raises questions about the meaning and content of messages in health crisis communication, specifically in the face of diverse social representations. The creation of musical content which should relate to sensitizing the African populations against Covid-19 requires us to identify the true meaning behind the commitment of African musical artists. We can do this by deciphering their significant works in communicating about the African public health crisis.

4.2.2. *Review and analysis of the corpus*

As mentioned above, the purpose of this study is to respond to concerns related to the production of musical works in Africa, in particular, to the forms of engagement of artists who are involved in disseminating information about the coronavirus disease on the black continent.

As an element of discourse and language, the qualitative method used when collecting the data was enunciative analysis and argumentative analysis, as defined by Charaudeau (2014). In the context of political discourse analysis, which serves as a model for musical discourse analysis, the enunciative analysis allowed us to highlight the locus aspects of artistic content. On the other hand, the argumentative analysis allowed us to highlight "the reasoning logics that characterize the ideological positioning" (Charaudeau 2014, p. 28) of this study population. These analyses covered 14 musical works from eight African countries since the beginning of this study in January 2020. Table 4.1 indicates a corpus of 14 items collected on digital social networks and primarily on the YouTube music application.

This digital platform is one of the social networks that African citizens, especially young people, use most often for video elements. They find video clips of artists, tutorials and films. Thus, YouTube music is part of the media perceived as a new generation of communication channels that compete with traditional media and present new informational issues, according to Castells (2013). All in all, this electronic source of musical information was of great help in collecting the information summarized below.

Author	Country of origin	Title of the song	Musical genre
Koffi Olomidé	DRC (Congo)	Corona assassin	Rumba
Magic Diézel	Ivory Coast	Coronavirus	Zouglou
Nouaman Lahlou	Morocco	Coronavirus	World music
Smarty	Burkina Faso	Alerte coron (Corona alert)	Hip-hop/rap
Fally Ipoupa	Congo Brazzaville	En mode confinement (In lockdown mode)	Rumba
Angelique Kidjo	Benin	No Pata	World music
Ferré Gola	DRC (Congo)	We're fighting corona virus, stop Covid-19	World music
Bobi Wine and Nubian Li	Uganda	Corona virus alert	Reggae
Aya Nakamura	Mali	Ho corona	R&B
Youssou N'Dour and Daan	Senegal	Stop corona	World music
The student Feat Placide Konan	Ivory Coast	A qui la faute (Whose fault is it)	Rap
Wally Seck	Senegal	Digglé	Pop music
Ndlovu youth choir	South Africa	We've got this fight against Coronavirus/Covid-19	Hip Hop
Collectif 236	Central African Republic	Covid-19 Tiri Ti î La	Rap

Table 4.1. *Summary table of data from the research corpus. Source: Table from the survey corpus*

This table includes information about the titles of the songs collected, the authors, their country of origin and the musical genres of the songs in question. All these data has allowed us to understand better the arguments' content, the meaning of the messages and the artists' objectives. The analysis and interpretation of the musical creations we collected from March to April 2020 at the Covid-19 crisis communications event are presented below.

4.3. Musical works for health prevention

4.3.1. *Health awareness and music creation in Africa*

Since the outbreak of the Coronavirus disease in Africa, crisis communication by most governments, medical authorities and institutional leaders has focused on a variety of decisions to observe restrictive measures and raise awareness about the threats posed by the disease. The strategies adopted by decision-makers should, in other words, encourage the population to adopt the almost universal gestures and restrictive measures in the fight against Covid-19 in public places. By doing so, authorities intended to protect their citizens by changing their behavior. This required exceptional leadership in the countries concerned to help ensure compliance with health requirements so that citizens could be protected.

According to the site Abidjan.net, in Côte d'Ivoire, for example, the speech made by the director of the Center for Information and Government Communication (*Centre d'information et de communication gouvernementale*, CICG) (05/06/2020) states that:

> Since the occurrence of the Coronavirus, crisis communication at the governmental level has not weakened. Various tools and actions are in place to make people aware of the danger of the disease, protect themselves, and change their behavior to contain the pandemic. [...] crisis communication is doing well, thanks to the strong leadership of the President of the Republic and the government.

According to national realities, various crisis communication strategies have been adopted to raise awareness among the population, more generally in line with the World Health Organization (WHO) recommendations. The fight against the pandemic has almost taken Africa and the world by surprise and involves decision-makers and individual civic responsibility. According to the South African President Cyril Ramaphosa, who also chairs the African Union (AU), the new phase in the fight against the virus will determine the fate of the South African nation, primarily through the actions of its people (Backman 2020). What he means is that people must gain a sense of responsibility.

Transmitting sensitization messages through music to help break an increasing flow of people who become positive for Covid-19 has emerged as a suitable way of circulating information to populations, considering the diversity of communication channels within the African media space.

The power of music as an instrument for disseminating information has not left African political leaders indifferent. They endeavor to encourage as many of their fellow citizens as possible to change their behavior toward Covid-19. According to Franceinfo and AFP (2020) in their online article entitled "Liberia: President George Weah sings against the coronavirus", published on March 25 2020, Liberia's President George Weah created music as an instrument to sensitize the Liberian populations through a song entitled "Let stand together and fight Coronavirus". Following the example of the Liberian President, who intended to make his awareness messages more effective through communication channels that are more accessible to the general population, according to the French daily newspaper *Le Monde* (2020), the Ethiopian government's Ministry of Health created a playlist of songs entitled "Video: in Africa, the fight against the coronavirus is made with music", and also decided to make some of these video clips musical, such as "Corona best comedy", a humorous 2 hour 3 mininute clip, which aims to arouse the sensibility of the Ethiopians on the issue of prevention against Covid-19.

Overall, Africa has used music (Trétarre 2012) in its communication strategies to encourage broad adhesion of social strata in its territory to the fight against the Covid-19 pandemic. Professionals in the music world have also been called upon (after being asked or by their own volition) to leverage their status as leaders to raise awareness among music lovers. Musical communication has therefore helped to set social standards.

4.3.2. *Music as a medium for raising health awareness*

Beyond governmental communications and public and private institutions, the creation of music in Africa has emerged as a new social sphere that has invested in the public medical sphere (Paillart 1995) in the fight against Covid-19. Whether in a controlled fashion or not, it has entered communications around the health crisis caused by the spread of the coronavirus pandemic in the world as well as in Africa. Even though it may not have moved away from denouncing social shifts as a mode of engagement during this sanitary crisis, the flow of information conveyed by the music has given way to modes of reconstructing the standard messages conceived by the national and international public authorities. Music has become a measure and restrictive gesture that has universal recommendations. These recommendations include frequent hand washing, keeping a spatial distance of 1 m from others, avoiding touching eyes, nose and mouth, respecting respiratory hygiene, and wearing protective masks. Other recommendations are state-specific and based on the State's socioeconomic and political realities. Other health security measures such as curfews, the creation of screening centers, the closure of public places (bars, markets, places of worship, etc.), quarantine of those who are sick, isolation of the most affected cities, closure of land and air borders, etc., have constituted the menu of response measures against Coronavirus in Africa.

However, complying with measures in a continent like Africa with multidimensional problems has not always been straightforward. Indeed, digital information has invaded Africa, much of which is considered fake news (Abidjan.net 2020). Streams of fake news contribute to the construction of social beliefs counterproductive to health security guidelines being followed on the continent. Behavioral inconsistencies within governmental or institutional discourses or strategies on various issues around protection contribute to the doubts that African populations have regarding the possible rise of Covid-19 in their daily lives. In this midst of a social world largely fed by social networks and channels that peddle information, music is intended to reinforce the health messages disseminated to citizens. In this way, it becomes a subtle aid to facilitate the transmission of health information and has emerged as a complement to public communication strategies. For this purpose, it covers a plethora of social representations and discourses to captivate the attention of "fans" by revealing prevailing social and health realities.

Under various musical genres (Zouglou, R&B, rumba, world music, reggae, Hip Hop, Pop music, rap, etc.), artists from various African countries well known to their national and international audiences have used their talent to cement health prevention messages for Covid-19.

Therefore, Ugandans Bobi Wine and Nubian Li use the reggae music genre to create a work called "Corona Virus Alert", which is written in English in the following terms:

The bad news is that everyone is a potential victim, but the good news is that everyone is a potential solution. Educate the masses about sanitation. Keep a social distance and stay self-contained. The Coronavirus is spreading worldwide... everyone must be vigilant.

The artists invite their fellow citizens to be more responsible when considering the disease. Maintaining the same prevention style, the musician Ferré Gola from the Democratic Republic of Congo (DRC) created a song called "We're fighting coronavirus, stop Covid-19", which demands that we fight the virus as much as possible to stop it in its tracks. The South African group "Ndlovu youth choir" claims to be able to defeat the Coronavirus in their song "We've got this fight against Coronavirus/Covid-19". They ask people not to panic and especially not to spread rumors. This group insists particularly on the principle of washing hands properly, which is one of the main suggestions of international and national institutions.

Most of the music that appeared during the coronavirus crisis reflects the recommendations of national and international institutions on measures and barriers to the fight against Covid-19. Music thus constitutes a means of sensitization against an uplifting backdrop and can, in this sense, convey messages which feel more accessible to the social strata or urban and rural communities. Koffi Olomidé with his song "Corona assassin", Aya Nakamoura with her song "Ho Corona", as well as many other African music stars such as Youssou N'Dour and Daan in Senegal, the Moroccan Nouaman Lahlou, using various musical genres have leveraged melody as action, turning it into an instrument to push forward the campaign of sensitization amongst African populations, hidden under dancing rhythms.

In the same vein as inviting African populations to put a stop to Covid-19 through music, Beninese artist Angélique Kidjo has released a new version of South African Miriam Makeba's hit "Pata Pata" ("touch touch touch" in the Xhosa language). With "No Pata Pata", the Beninese star advises people to stay at home and avoid physical contact with each other.

These musical works by African artists in the coronavirus health context reveal subjectively constructed lyrics and statements that can bring about changes in behavior. Because of their aesthetic characteristics and the pleasure they provide at the level of hearing, music differs from ordinary prescriptive discourse to position itself as a popular channel to disseminate messages, particularly health messages in the present context of the Covid-19 epidemic. Therefore, African leaders in the culture industry use melodies to raise awareness among their fellow citizens. This shows a commitment through which they express their opinions in parallel with the sensitization of individuals to respect the recommended measures and restrictive actions. Musical works by African singer-artists on the current health environment reveal, to paraphrase Achard (2011, p. 157), statements that are subjective, to say the least, but which have the power to manipulate opinions, even directing them toward the desired direction as a "committed medium", by raising awareness of or criticizing society's flaws.

4.3.3. *The issue of health governance in creating music*

The songs released in Africa in the context of the fight against Coronavirus on the continent are characterized by the words crafted, on the one hand. They accompany the strategies of prevention campaigns adopted by the African elites influenced by international recommendations.

On the other hand, the words are characterized by their denunciation of the flaws in managing crisis communication by public health actors, including, first and foremost, governments. These criticisms refer, of course, to the shortcomings in managing the health crisis and the false information (or fake news) to which a large part of the African population has been exposed through direct or indirect contact with digital social media networks.

This issue of the invasion of fake news has not been insignificant in the eyes of African elites, who have not hesitated to denounce it as a concern. According to Backman (2020), many African personalities, including the Heads of State, have denounced this information, which is harmful to the health action plans drawn up in the fight against Covid-19. Gabonese President Ali Bongo is said to have decided to act against "those who spread outrageous alarmist messages" (Backman 2020). According to the journalist, the same was true for Chadian President Idriss Déby, who warned the perpetrators of criminal practices on the Internet after having estimated that "social networks, instead of disseminating information from good sources, which are authentic and verified, indulge in misinformation and manipulation, thus sowing doubt, panic and paranoia" among the population (Backman 2020).

Other countries, such as Burkina Faso and Côte d'Ivoire, have taken on this denunciation strategy in the fight against false news. In this context of communicational action, the Burkinabe artist Smarty, under the title "Alerte Corona", did his musical work to denounce the propagator of public rumors and false news in his State, likely to undermine communication efforts undertaken. More specifically, Samarty reveals the following in his song:

> Rumors say that it is a white disease
> That Mamadou is the healer with his medicine
> Rumors say that it is a biological attack
> Mr. Rumor will eventually bury Africa
> Prevention is better than death in this context [...]

These words evoke paradigms that have fuelled street news about Covid-19. In his lyrics, the Burkinabé artist expresses his indignation at the informational power of rumor, which could lead Africa to its demise by creating a breeding ground for Coronavirus. Although they have served as communication channels for African elites, such as the Heads of State, in their strategies for approaching the population (Jeune Afrique 2020), social networks are the main vehicles for these rumors. This situation is alongside the circulation of rumors by "word of mouth", which must be translated from Ivorian slang as interpersonal or face-to-face communication.

Electronic media offers a broader possibility to make itself present on numerous platforms in perpetual creation. Regularly in contradiction with official information sources, false news, also known by the term fake news, embodies "the weapons of the false" (Huyghe 2016, p. 1) as key elements of misinformation. The effects of these rumors appear even more contagious as they amplify citizens' existing doubts and beliefs. This is a situation about which the vocal work of artists such as Smarty from Burkina Faso and others from the world of culture calls for awareness by arousing emotion. However, rumors are not the only ways to denounce illicit facts. Acts committed by political actors which are failures in the fight against the Covid-19 pandemic have also come under fire.

The Ivorian singer Placide Konan, using a rap style in his song *A qui la faute* (Whose fault is it?), protests against the practices and behaviors of the Ivorian political authorities that he believes are in contradiction with preventive measures and gestures that they have recommended. Indeed, in Côte d'Ivoire, 2020 is the year of the presidential elections as defined by the constitution for each 5-year term. It is also a period of political development in a tense climate considering the conquest or conservation of state power. The fight against Covid-19 has appeared there, as in many other countries, as a means of political recuperation, in which those in power and their supporters defy the safety instructions with impunity, such as a ban on popular gatherings of more than 50 people, physical distancing measures, self-isolation.

Based on these observations, the words of the singer's denunciation are expressed in these terms:

> [...] we thought it was everyone's business and not that of one camp
> All these awareness campaigns were put to death when the king shook hands with his son at the airport
> In this pandemic, some are rich, and the poor
> There are those we kill, and there are the others
> Error is human but to remain in error hides unhealthy realities
> [...]
> October 31 is not far [...]

The lyrics of denunciation appear here as if the artist is angry at governmental authorities who seem to have decided on measures and restrictive actions for one part of the population. The artist also denounces commercial activities that are exempt from prevention measures. The message that emerges from this song is a cry from deep within the artist. He denounces the management system put in place by the Ivorian political power. The author wants a change in the management mode and consequently a change at the head of the State, shown in his reference: "October 31 is not far", which constitutes the day for voting for the next candidate in the presidential election of 2020. The artist brings out a unique tone and a musical genre highlighting the problems that undermine the proper management of communication for disease prevention. In this context, in Africa, several musical rhythms are used to denounce or relate the social realities experienced daily by the people.

4.4. Conclusion

4.4.1. *The Covid-19 crisis in Africa: a prevention emergency*

The rapid spread of Covid-19 has upset all social, economic, political and health forecasts in the world and has positioned itself as a major public health issue. Detected in Wuhan (China) and declared in March 2020 by the World Health Organization (WHO) as a global pandemic, the Coronavirus has defied all forms of "superpower" to impose itself in governance and management programs across all territories. This sanitary environment has thus propelled a general mobilization of the population and the public powers in the form of decisions being made and restrictive measures being observed, which have constrained global populations but have been necessary for the survival of humanity which faces the devastating effects of a microvirus.

In short, faced with the need to respond as quickly and urgently as possible, health news has not run out of information to disseminate. Preventive measures have been taken everywhere: restrictive measures (physical distancing, hand washing), more stringent protection measures against the disease (quarantine of populations, curfews, etc.), scientific collaborations and various forms of crisis communication among political authorities, institutional and community leaders.

4.4.2. *Music as a communication medium for health*

Musical creation in Africa focuses on disseminating melodious information about the dangers of the Coronavirus pandemic. Dancing is a manifestation of emotion, using a variety of sound instruments such as tom-toms, balafons and various media from the traditions of the peoples of Africa. It remains a practice widely shared among populations. The circulation of this musical information is also promoted by traditional media and by a new generation of media channels constituted by digital social networks (Facebook, Twitter, Instagram, Snapchat, Whatsapp, etc.), audio and video streaming platforms and services (iTunes, Spotify, Deezer, Youtube, Netflix, etc.), which profoundly change the way music is consumed, videos are viewed and multimedia information is shared and accessed (Tchéhouali 2016, pp. 4–5). Musical creations have several currents, whether in terms of past songs and more modern creations of the current generation. The social actors exposed to these works of artistic production are mostly young people between 15 and 25 years old. They are young people addicted to music and films, which they can usually download via YouTube, Netflix or other platforms.

Moreover, the musical environment in the African continent, rich and dynamic in its cultural diversity, has many talented singers and groups. Music that raises social awareness of the dangers of Covid-19 and behavior change includes content that invites people to comply with restrictive gestures and lyrics that challenge disrespectful attitudes. As a crucial component of cultural identity, music is a familiar and necessary medium to transmit information.

Regarding communication for behavior change and toward the risks incurred by the public in the spread of Covid-19, African music, which has multiple modern currents and of various generations, has appropriate awareness campaigns. Thus, the sensitization of the African populations to the dangers of the coronavirus disease will have other actors emerging aside from the official authorities because of the profile of the stars in the world of the culture industry.

They have played their part in setting up the media as a tool to fight against Covid-19. Their messages, constructed and disseminated for this purpose, appear, for the most part, as information which relays the measures and restrictive actions to be complied with to fight against Covid-19. In this period of awareness raising through music, some musical artists have conveyed criticism of the governance led by African leaders to boost the disease outside their territory. In contrast, others have been more interested in denouncing public rumors and the communication networks that support them.

Through the facts that can be observed since the outbreak of the coronavirus health crisis in Africa, this study has allowed us to understand that music, aside from its aesthetic vocation to offer sensory and auditory delight (Bohui 2009), is a powerful means of raising awareness of the risks that are linked to the spread of Covid-19 on the African continent. Through its entertaining nature, it also constitutes a tool for denouncing poor governance. Engaged music is, therefore, part of a crisis communication dynamic; it serves as a channel for transmitting information to raise civic awareness. Social media platforms such as YouTube music, ones less prone to censorship, are now the main channels for disseminating these entertaining messages.

4.5. References

Achard, G. (2011), *La com' au pouvoir : le nouveau langage des politiques et des médias enfin décrypté !* Fyp Éditions, Paris.

Bohui, H. (2009). Un opprimé danse, chante : la musique comme moyen de lutte. *Médias et crises en Afrique : Forum*. Revue des Arts et de la Communication, No. 1 spécial, Abidjan.

Castells, M. (2013). *Communication et pouvoir*. Éditions de la maison des sciences de l'homme, Paris.

Dedi, S.F. (1985). Hommage à Ernesto Djédjé. *Kasa Bya Kasa. Revue africaine d'Anthropologie et de Sociologie*, no. 5, Abidjan.

Gaulier, A. (2015). Chansons de France, chansons de l'immigration maghrébine. Étude de l'album Origines contrôlées. *Afrique contemporaine*, 254, 73–87.

Goran, K.M. and Adigran, J.-P. (2009). Crise africaine et création musicale. *Médias et crises en Afrique : Forum. Revue des Arts et de la Communication*, no. 1 spécial, Abidjan.

Huyghe, F.-B. (2016). *La désinformation : les armes du faux*. Armand Colin, Paris.

Kolé, S.M. and Adou, S.E. (2019). La migration à travers la musique urbaine ivoirienne. *Revue communication en question*, Abidjan [Online]. Available at: http://www.comenquestion.com/ [Accessed 20 January 2020].

Libaert, T. (2010). *La communication de crise*. Dunod, Paris.

Mucchielli, A. (2001). *Les sciences de l'information et de la communication*, 3rd edition. Hachette, Paris.

Paillart, I. (1995). *L'espace public et l'emprise de la communication*. Université Grenoble Alpes, Éditions Ellug, Grenoble.

Tchehouali, D. (2016). Étude sur les enjeux et les retombées économiques et artistiques de la diffusion et la distribution en ligne de contenu culturel ACP. Programme UE-ACP d'appui au secteur culturel. Programme du Groupe des Etats ACP. Union européenne. 10ème Fonds Européen de Développement, Final Report.

Tretarre, F. (2012). *Campagnes électorales : principes et pratiques de la préparation et de la conduite de campagnes.* Gualino éditeur, Paris.

Wondji, C. (ed.) (1986). *La Chanson populaire en Côte-d'Ivoire : essai sur l'art de Gabriel Srolou.* Présence Africaine, Paris.

Online resources

Abidjan.net (2020). Coronavirus – Bakary Sanogo (Directeur du CICG) : "La Communication de crise est facilitée par le leadership fort du gouvernement dans la gestion de la crise" [Online]. Available at: https://news.abidjan.net/h/674042.html [Accessed 5 August 2020].

Backman, F. (2020). Covid-19 en Afrique : Aïd el Fitr, virus et messages présidentiels. Fondation Jean-Jaurès [Online]. Available at: https://jean-jaures.org/nos-productions/covid-19-en-afrique-aid-el-fitr-virus-et-messages-presidentiels [Accessed 22 July 2020].

Franceinfo and AFP (2020). Liberia : le président Georges Weah chante contre le coronavirus [Online]. Available at: https://www.francetvinfo.fr/monde/afrique/societe-africaine/liberia-le-president-george-weah-chante-contre-le-coronavirus_3885653.html [Accessed 16 August 2020].

Jeune Afrique (2020). Coronavirus : quand les chefs d'État africains font dans la prévention [Online]. Available at: https://www.jeuneafrique.com/927182/politique/en-images-coronavirus-quand-les-chefs-detat-africains-font-dans-la-prevention/ [Accessed 19 August 2020].

Le Monde Afrique (2020). Vidéo : en Afrique, la lutte contre le coronavirus se fait en musique [Online]. Available at: https://www.lemonde.fr/afrique/video/2020/04/17/video-en-afrique-la-lutte-contre-le-coronavirus-se-fait-en-musique_6036975_3212.html [Accessed 16 August 2020].

Le Point d'Afrique (2020). Bilan. La crise sanitaire du Covid-19 va coûter très cher à l'Afrique [Online]. Available at: https://www.rfi.fr/fr/afrique/20200518-covid-19-la-riposte-institutions-africaines-coronavirus [Access 22 July 2020].

RFI (2020). Coronavirus : la riposte des institutions africaines [Online]. Available at: https://www.rfi.fr/fr/afrique/20200518-covid-19-la-riposte-institutions-africaines-coronavirus [Accessed 15 July 2020].

5

Rethinking Theatrical Performances in the Covid-19 Era: Strategies and Perspectives

In addition to being a way to express literature, the theater is an activity characterized by performing on stage to entertain, educate or sensitize people gathered in a given place and at a specific time. In the face of Covid-19, the essential functions of the theater were disrupted due to restrictive measures. Thus, the theater needs to be redesigned to continue producing theatrical productions and relieve the pain experienced by populations caused by the disease. The theater may then be reinvented and adapted to the new situation in which we find ourselves. The theater has attempted to survive by producing shows using various communication tools while strictly respecting the measures in place. The themes contained within theatrical performances are essentially oriented toward prevention, therapy and public health to help populations to become aware of and overcome the difficulties linked to the pandemic.

5.1. Introduction

Covid-19 is a disease that was discovered in December 2019 in the city of Wuhan, China. According to WHO, it is an acute respiratory syndrome caused by SARS-CoV-2[1]. On March 11, 2020, the first contamination case was identified and confirmed in Côte d'Ivoire, which disrupted all activities. "There is no sector of activity [...] that is not affected by the restrictive health measures taken by the Government" (Kamaté 2020, p. 395).

Chapter written by Losséni FANNY.

1 Severe acute respiratory syndrome Coronavirus 2.

The artistic and cultural sector has not been spared. Restrictive measures have slowed or even halted theatrical performances altogether due to periods of lockdowns, closures of venues and social distancing. However, theatrical performances must survive in social, economic and political situations; as a source of resilience, they are indispensable to humanity. They contribute to education, enrichment and physical and mental well-being. These different observations give rise to the following research topic: "rethinking theatrical representations in the era of Covid-19: strategies and perspectives".

The word "rethink", suggests that it is imperative to think deeply to find strategies, that is to say, a set of coordinated actions and skillful operations, to allow for the production of theatrical representations in this period of a health crisis. The notion of "theatrical representation", according to Pavis (2006, p. 302), "insists on the idea of a representation of something that already exists [...] before being embodied on a stage". It extends to how scenes are set up, that is, how dramatic texts are transformed into scenic representations, which take shape in the presence of the public whose observation characterizes the spectacle. It led N'Gandu to state that theatrical practice evolves with strong relations between the characters on stage, insofar as those characters only exist because of the entire operation between the public and the spectator. Covid-19 spreads very fast in public. With this in mind, it is necessary to rethink theatrical representations so that they can be adapted to the new situation.

How can we rethink theatrical performances? What strategies are needed to be able to do this? For what purposes should theatrical performances be rethought?

Our objective is to show that theater professionals are trying to reinvent theater to withstand the health crisis. To do this, we will use a sociological method to collect technical data through a survey, interviews and documentation. The survey and interviews will be conducted on a sample of three people, extracted from a target population composed of theater professionals. Our work will be structured around three main points. The first point will briefly present the state of Ivorian theatrical performances before Covid-19, the second will analyze the situation of theatrical performances during Covid-19 and the third will explore their resilience and resistance.

5.2. Brief status of Ivorian theatrical performances before Covid-19

Before the advent of Covid-19, theatrical representations in Côte d'Ivoire had their glory days from 1970 to 1990. After this period, the evolution of theater productions slowed due to difficulties.

5.2.1. *The glory years of theatrical performances*

Since its birth in the colonial schools of Bingerville and Wiliam Ponty in Dakar, Ivorian theater evolved until it reached its peak in the 1970s. Since that time, Ivorian theater has seen some great actors. Names like Adjé Daniel, Bienvenue Neba, Diallo Ticouai Vincent, Bity Moro, Gondo Pierre and Thérèse Tabah are still fresh in our memories.

These actors were constantly performing in packed theaters. At that time, every Saturday, the major cultural centers of Abidjan and Bouaké scheduled theatrical performances. Thus, the Jacques Aka cultural center in Bouaké, the Théâtre de la Cité in Cocody and the French cultural center in Plateau were packed every weekend with the people who love this type of art[2].

In addition to being a distraction, the theater was a means of education for Ivorians because it allowed them to understand more about their lives. As Shakespeare once said, "For any thing so o'erdone is from the purpose of playing, whose end, both at the first and now, was and is, to hold as 'twere the mirror up to nature: to show virtue her feature, scorn her own image, and the very age and body of the time his form and pressure" (Hamlet, Shakespeare).

Thus, through performances such as "Adama champion" by Kotéba, Souleymane Koly dramatized the misadventure of a talented footballer called Adama, who went into exile to pursue a career in soccer. Unfortunately, he returns home with a double fracture, ending his

---

[2] Available at: http://ampoproduction.over-blog.com/2020/02/les-annees-de-gloire-du-theatre-ivoirien.html.

ambitions. Similarly, the theatrical performances entitled "les mangeurs de poulets crevés", "les mains vides" and "Adjati" directed by Adjé Daniel were satirical about society.

In 1980–1990, to promote the theater, Ivorian television showed a program called "Theatre at home", which projected a theatrical performance every Thursday. Aminata Ouattara, a drama teacher and theater enthusiast, remembers this beautiful time in these terms:

> Côte d'Ivoire had renowned theater companies. Despite our young age, we did not want to miss any of their theatrical representation broadcast on the Ivorian television channel because all the plays were of good quality and were worth watching[3].

Theater being shown on TV has meant that the general public has been exposed to talented actors like Zoumana, Gbizié Troupa Bruno, Fargas Assandé and Kouadio Ephrasie. Zoumana and Fargas Assandé began acting with the school theatre, and they have been propelled onto the national and international scene. People still remember the awards won by the Divo high school because of these two famous actors. The theater's glory was set to suffer gradually from the 1990s onwards.

5.2.2. *Theatrical performances facing difficulties*

The term "difficulty" comes in response to those claiming that Ivorian theater is dead. Contrary to what laypeople may think, Ivorian theater is not defunct, and although it is certainly not in great shape, it continues to survive. Koné Wagninlba Jocelyn[4] further says that despite problems, "the Ivorian theater is doing well. Those who say that the theater is dead, in reality, do not go to the theater. But it is important to recognize that Ivorian theater has been suffering for some time".

Indeed, after its heyday, Ivorian theater, which has uncovered renowned actors, began encountering huge problems. From 1990, theatrical

---

3 Interview with Ouattara Aminata, drama teacher at the Institut National Supérieur des Arts et de l'Action Culturelle (INSAAC).
4 Koné Wagninlba Jocelyn is the Artistic Director of the National Theater and Dance Company (*Compagnie Nationale de Théâtre et de Danse*) at the *Centre National des Arts et de la Culture* (CNAC) in Côte d'Ivoire. We interviewed him on Monday, January 24, 2022.

performances started to become rarely shown on television. Over time, theaters transformed into places of worship. The cost of renting the spaces that still exist is exorbitant.

As the years go by, talented actors become idle, while others like Adjé Daniel die. Many of them languish under the shadow of age and poverty. The cries from the heart of theatre professionals do not concern the authorities in charge of culture. In the past, Diallo Ticouaï Vincent launched an appeal to the government in his role as Director of Cocody theater. But this appeal was disregarded. Due to this, he organized leisure days that aimed to boost the presence of the theater. Lovers of this art form came out in large numbers. They attended in their masses the theatrical performances produced by theatre companies. Adjé Daniel attended a performance despite his deteriorating health. Amazed by the talent of young actors, he called on the authorities to be attentive to the concerns of theater professionals. Diallo Ticouai Vincent took the opportunity to write a piece he submitted to the Minister of Culture and Francophonie. Unfortunately, nothing was done in response. The lack of a real policy to alleviate the theater's problems and encourage the next generation has pushed talented young people like Adama Dahico, Omega David and Adrienne Koutouan to opt for humor and to convert to the cinema, argues Ouattara Aminata[5].

The Palace of Culture in Treichville, built and inaugurated on October 1, 1999, has been a source of relief for the theater. It hosts major shows such as the MASA[6], during which theater groups are selected to perform. Unfortunately, renting this architectural gem is expensive for the theater professional. "For a show, the cost of renting varies between 300,000 Fr and 400,000 Fr Cfa, which is too much for actors", says Ouattara Aminata[7]. Following the Ivorian crisis of 2010–2011, this space has been heavily damaged, looted and ransacked, increasing the problems faced by the theater. Following this observation, Maurice Kouakou Bandaman, Minister of Culture and Francophonie, made a series of promises during the celebration of World Theater Day in 2012. According to Abidjan.net, he said that Ivorian theater would not die because the Head of State, Alassane Ouattara, has ensured that all the arts, including theater, will regain their

---

5 Interview with Ouattara Aminata, conducted on January 21, 2022.
6 Abidjan Arts and Entertainment Market.
7 Ouattara Aminata, *op. cit.*

noble letters[8]. The construction of new theaters had been announced. Unfortunately, this promise has also remained unfulfilled. This is why Tapé Ernest[9] summarizes by saying that the difficulties of the theater are related to a lack of political will in Côte d'Ivoire. The health crisis of 2019 can be added to all of these difficulties combined to test the theater. With the closure of venues, losses accumulate and the prospects of the theater remain unclear.

5.3. The situation of theatrical performances during Covid-19

Covid-19 has had an impact on Ivorian theater. According to Koné Wagninlba Jocelyn[10], the consequences have been both negative and positive.

5.3.1. *The negative effects of Covid-19 on theatrical performances*

The negative effects of Covid-19 on the creative and cultural sector in Côte d'Ivoire can be presented in terms of losses. The spread of the pandemic has badly impacted this sector. The consequences have been more visible since the Ivorian government decided to take additional measures to deal with the pandemic. These measures have affected the theatre considerably. We are witnessing total cancellation of shows: no more theatrical performances or gatherings of spectators. Four of the twelve recommendations imposed by the Ivorian State strongly threaten the creative and cultural sector. These are as follows:

– the closure of nightclubs, cinemas and entertainment venues for a renewable period of 15 days;

– the suspension of all national and international sports and cultural events for a renewable period of 15 days;

– the respect of a distance of at least 1 m between people in big spaces, maquis, restaurants, company offices, airport zones and public places;

---

8 Les news.abidjan.net, available at: https://news.abidjan.net/articles.
9 A manager of a national theater company in Côte d'Ivoire.
10 Interview with Koné Wagninlba Jocelyn, conducted on January 24, 2022.

– the prohibition of population gatherings of more than 50 people for a renewable period of 15 days.

Some of these recommendations have been renewed several times, but others remain, leading to the further demise of theaters and venues already suffering. Thus, cultural centers in the country and the Palace of Culture in Abidjan, which is supposed to host or organize theatrical performances, have remained closed for a long time.

Despite the opening of some venues, social distancing measures remain an obstacle to theatrical performances because they restrict the public and limit financial gains. In this sense, Abdelkébir Rgagna agrees, explaining that: "the coronavirus was a real obstacle for theater professionals since theaters have also been closed. Added to this is that the theater is a living art that cannot be projected on digital platforms".

The implications of the recommendations are social, economic and political, and they affect the social rights of cultural professionals and the protection of the diversity of cultural expressions. Some people, such as Adjé Daniel, have found themselves in economic insecurity and psychological instability. On this subject, Koné Wagninlba Jocelyn said:

> The sanitary crisis related to Covid-19 has been a great obstacle for the theater. It was a danger for the psychology of the professionals working in this art and citizens. It has had negative social impacts on the actors. It was unimaginable to know that many actors live daily and do not have other stable activities. So, with the spread of the pandemic, life has stopped for many of them since even the status of being an artist does not protect them.

These statements show that Covid-19 seriously threatens theater professionals who deplore the loss of several contracts, including canceling scheduled theatrical performances. This was the case of the play *La fille du Bistrot* by Alma production, which was set to be held at Boz'art[11] in Abidjan in May 2020. The *Institut Français de Côte d'Ivoire* (IFCI) had planned to organize an evening called *La soirée de dénonciation des violences faites aux femmes* (An evening to denounce violence against women) with Nash

---

11 Name of a performance space in Abidjan.

featuring in the program. During this evening, the show *Le voile se déchire* (The Veil is Torn) by the theater company Dumanlé, which was to be held, was canceled. Similarly, the theater company Ivoire Marionnette's tour, which was to be held in Belgium as part of the large French program *Africa 20.20*, was canceled.

The show *Fuenté Obejuna*, directed by Vagba Obou De Sales and Louis Marques from Alma production, which was to be held in some European countries in May and June 2020, was canceled. The theater was now being recreated on social networks. But according to Koné Wagninlba Jocelyn, the human connection that the theater provides in person tends to disappear when it comes to digital theater. Without the public, all the life that animates the theater disappears.[12]

As can be seen, the additional recommendations adopted by the State of Côte d'Ivoire to combat Covid-19 have prevented the production of theatrical performances and favored the digitization of theater. Lifting these additional measures depends on how the health situation unfolds. Unfortunately, new contamination cases and variants, such as the omicron virus, are announced daily in the media. This implies that Covid-19 continues to threaten the population on a national and international scale. But this disease has not been only negative for theater professionals. Some of them have used it as an opportunity.

5.3.2. Positive effects of Covid-19 on theatrical performances

Talking about the positive effects of a health crisis on the production of theatrical performances may seem incongruous. It should be mentioned from the outset that the positive effects we are talking about here mainly surround the creative spirit that the disease has stimulated in the shadows and the resourcefulness of professionals to find ways to reinvent their craft. They have first applied the process of distancing themselves from reality. Salma Mokhtar Amanat Allah affirms this effect:

> We knew creativity requires a priori mental clarity, which was not available because of this incomprehensible world problem.

---

12 Koné Wagninlba Jocelyn, *op. cit.*

We first had to step back and understand what was happening around us. After this stage, we started understanding the situation and getting used to coexisting with it without returning to normal life.

For the latter, the Coronavirus has been a real catalyst for creativity. Some artists, like Koné Wagninlba Jocelyn, took advantage of the lockdown to prepare their works. In his words:

> The periods of lockdown became sources of inspiration. During these moments, theater people took advantage of them to work behind the scenes, which meant they could perform theatrical performances after the lockdown. I took the opportunity to prepare a production on the theme of immigration during the lockdown period, which I presented in high schools and performance spaces after lockdown.[13]

This period also favored the creation of a theatrical project called *Les vendredis de L'ESTCA*[14] at INSAAC, which, today, consists of presenting a theatrical play every Friday evening starting at 6:30 PM in the Bitty Moro space.

Thus, from these examples, Abdelkébir Rgagna said that "this period we have lived through can give us inspiration for subjects to explore and put on stage, subjects we had never even thought of"[15]. These same comments are supported by Azzopardi (2020), for whom the health crisis linked to Covid-19 "is an interesting period for creation, conducive to reflecting on society and our consumption model".

In the case of Covid-19, the theater does not present ordinary, gratuitous or private situations; it represents social facts that are close to the people and can help them overcome the crisis. And this is what justifies its resilience and its need to resist pressures to collapse.

---

13 Interview conducted on Saturday, January 22, 2022 with Souleymane Sow, Ivorian director and teacher of theater at the *Institut National Supérieur des Arts et de l'Action Culturelle* (INSAAC).
14 The ESTCA is the *École Supérieur de théâtre, de Cinéma et d'Audiovisuel* housed at the INSAAC.
15 Abdelkébir Rgagna, *op. cit.*

5.4. Theatrical representations: resilience and resistance

As theater is the art by which man's actions are imitated, artistic comedians are always inspired by current events to represent reality and educate, relieve and amuse. The theater thus becomes an art form that "aims to educate its audience, inviting them to reflect on a problem, to understand a situation or to adopt a certain moral or political attitude" (Pavis 2006, p. 372). These qualities of the theater are essential to the well-being of humanity, and its physical and mental balance, especially in times of crisis. So, the theater is obligated to resist this period of health crisis. In doing so, the theater can become a source of social resilience.

5.4.1. *Theatrical performances as a source of social resilience during Covid-19*

When strictly complying with restrictive measures, using communication channels, and mobilizing public authorities, theatre productions may appear as strategies through which the theater may adapt to the new situation created by Covid-19. These strategies can help the theater become a source of social resilience.

5.4.1.1. The resilience of theatrical representations based on communication channels

At the beginning of Covid-19, theater professionals descended into chaos. However, they eventually took a step back to evaluate the situation and quickly put in place a structure due to which they could allow theatrical performances to take place and be watched. New methods and practices are being adopted based on communication channels and respect for measures to allow the theater to access its fans. As Koné Wagninlba Jocelyn says: "Covid-19 has allowed us to be resilient, to find new solutions that consist in digitizing the theater, in presenting it on social networks. The theater has recovered new spaces to escape the fury of the pandemic".

Thus, the pandemic has allowed the theater to reinvent itself, using communication channels to relay theatrical performances. The theater now circulates on television, radio, WhatsApp, Facebook, Instagram and Youtube. These communication channels try to maintain the constant relationship between the audience-spectator and virtual or theatrical performances.

Souleymane Sow[16] agreed when he said that in 2021 Alma production used digital means to make theater where radio is recorded. He cites the example of the recording of a play that raises awareness of the methods of farming coffee cocoa in the west of Côte d'Ivoire. Similarly, he maintains that the project of rehearsing and performing an improvisation show in Belgium in February 2021 with the participation of Côte d'Ivoire was adapted into an online program.

Close observation shows that communication channels participate significantly in safeguarding the Côte d'Ivoire theater during this health crisis period. Through social networks, actors spread prevention messages to fight against the spread of the virus. Koné Wagninlba Jocelyn gives the example of the famous comedian Kôrô Abou, whom Internet users can find through his web TV channel, who takes a serious situation like Covid-19 and makes fun of it. In a comedy, the actor sells mufflers that he asks the customer to try before buying. He tries and discards each muffler because he claims not to like any of them. This scene presents a ridiculous situation, yet it aims to moralize the public on the importance of covering one's nose. A nose cover is not something to try on before buying it; it is unique, according to Koné Wagninlba Jocelyn[17]. The actor thus transports the viewer into this visceral world to make those who have already done it see the error in their ways and to dissuade those who will be tempted to do it.

Thus, through communication channels, theatrical actors manage to change the mentality and behavior of the population regarding the seriousness of Covid-19. By accompanying the theater, communication channels succeed in making theatrical performances more positive and better, preparing them to persevere and become resilient for future generations.

5.4.1.2. *The resilience of theatrical performances based on compliance with restrictive measures*

With the lifting of the lockdown and the relaxation of additional measures, theatrical performances have become possible while respecting the measures still in force and that need to be upheld in the presence of the public spectator who comes to the theaters. Koné Wagninlba Jocelyn describes this period as the re-emergence of theatrical activities. According

---

16 Souleymane Sow, *op. cit.*
17 Koné Wagninlba Jocelyn, *op. cit.*

to him, this re-emergence took place in 2021, and he took the opportunity to produce his storytelling show ad prepared during the lockdown period. The storytelling and theater show was part of the CNAC's school and culture project. Thus, as he says: "we used the tale *Ambition amère* to produce a theatrical show, at the Lycée Mami Fêtê of Bingerville, at the Lycée jeune fille de Yopougon, at the CNAC café theatre, to sensitize young people when it comes to the topic of illegal immigration. This show teaches young people that the promised land is nowhere if it is not at home. The show was produced by strictly respecting social distancing, with a limited number of spectators sitting side by side, wearing masks to protect against disease. The show *Fuenté Obejuna*, directed by Vagba Obou De Sales and Louis Marques of Alma production, which was originally due to be held in some European countries in May and June 2020, was finally held in November 2021.

With these examples, it is undeniable that theater, as a source of resilience, aims to resist by adapting to the context of the health crisis and orienting the representations toward topics about human well-being. Therefore, theater appears as one of the effective means to fight against the disease. It is an instrument of public health that can relieve the trauma of populations and comfort the sick. There is a direct relationship between theatrical performances and psycho-social well-being. Faced with the general psychosis caused by Covid-19, the theater appears as a kind of therapy for the population. Its impact is a therapeutic process that allows the release of emotional and physical symptoms with the objective of greater personal well-being. Therefore, Vandevelde and Morhain (2012, p. 125) argue that "nowadays, the therapeutic and socializing dimension of group theater no longer needs to be demonstrated. Within psychiatric hospitals, patient theater groups are no longer an exception".

Dramatic performances provide many wellness benefits: social integration, unity, enjoyment, learning, meaning-making, self-actualization and well-being. In addition, playwrights can use a variety of dramatic expressions through entertainment to disseminate health information, encourage behavior change and promote public health recommendations.

The example of Kôrô Abou's play, which makes people laugh, shows that humanity should not continue to be alarmed by this crisis; it is often necessary to laugh about it because laughter is a source of mental well-being. Another example is Koné Wagninlba Jocelyn, who says he participated in a project called *Les consultations poétiques* in connection with the Paris theater, which is a kind of therapeutic theater where the actor plays the role of a doctor. He makes consultations and questions the public on the state of culture in general. Thus, as he states:

> This representation occurred in strategic places that welcomed the public regarding sanitary rules. We did it at the lagoon station of Treichville, the CNAC café theater, and some corners of the city of Abidjan. The Abidjanese public very well appreciated it. At the end of the performance, the actor gives the people advice and prescribes books to read for their well-being[18].

In this way, drama professionals engaged in the fight against Covid-19 with communities can help guide and relay the definition of a common vision and set goals so that people can feel socially safe. The theater appears as an innovative, creative and imaginative method to allow the public to develop their consciousness in this sensitive period by allowing them to question their pervading attitudes and behaviors.

Theater can facilitate collective rebuilding during Covid-19. Therapy messages can help policymakers understand the fundamental role of theater in sustainable and inclusive recovery from the throes of the health crisis. The resilient role of theatre promotes the psychological strengthening of communities that, when socially bonded, can recover fully or recover more quickly despite the crisis.

5.4.2. Prospects for theater in situations of a health crisis

All sectors need support in a crisis. Especially "with the Covid-19 pandemic, arts, and culture [...] need government support to mitigate the negative effects of containment and economic downturn, but also to accelerate the recovery process" (Sameh and Ottone 2020). In Côte d'Ivoire, support for the theater will be possible through interventions of the Ministry of Culture. In a document called CURE[19], published on December 12, 2018, the World Bank and UNESCO discussed that "The critical role that culture plays in planning and financing projects for cities affected by war and

---

18 Koné Wagninlba Jocelyn, *op. cit.*
19 CURE stands for Culture in City Reconstruction and Recovery. It is a document to be used for policy planning and project implementation for post-crisis (conflict and natural disaster) city reconstruction and recovery processes.

disasters when presenting a new policy paper *La culture dans la reconstruction et le relèvement des Villes, le November 16 (17 h 30) au siège de l'UNESCO"*.

This declaration also appears to be a commitment by the government to support the arts and cultural sector in its efforts to combat HIV through its awareness-raising messages. This general framework proposes principles and strategies that can be applied to the current situation as communities worldwide attempt to cope with and recover from the pandemic.

The Côte d'Ivoire must not sit outside this fundamental principle promoted by the CURE. The Ivorian State must invest in promoting the cultural and artistic sector by encouraging in-person performances directed toward behavior changes during this period of Covid-19. To do this, it must support cultural professionals with funding so that they can live and survive through their art. According to the director Souleymane Sow, nothing has been done in this sense: "I know that we have received a few kilos of rice and oil as aid from the Ministry of Youth and Employment".

This crisis should be seen as an opportunity for the Ivorian state to create a think tank that involves all theater professionals to help them resist possible future crises. Some professionals in this sector have already envisaged several prospects to create a better theatre practice during Covid-19. Koné Wagnilba Jocelyn, for example, proposes more action in open spaces, that is to say, to make theater in the streets, the soccer fields and the schoolyards, a bit like the forum theater already does. "It is this form of resilience that we are working toward", he concludes.

Like other people working in culture, many theater professionals use strategies to make theater more resilient and resistant in this health crisis. The state needs to listen more carefully to hear them.

5.5. Conclusion

At the end of this study, it should be noted that the health crisis related to the Covid-19 disease has slowed down all activities worldwide. The artistic and cultural field has not been spared in Côte d'Ivoire. The theater has been impacted both negatively and positively by the crisis. The negative impact comes from the theater being a living art. Therefore, theatrical performances require spaces provided for this purpose (room, open-air) with the physical presence of the public. Unfortunately, the protective measures against Covid-19 do not allow the theatre to take place effectively. Covid-19 has also been a source of inspiration and creativity for the actors during the lockdown. The effects of Covid-19 have made it possible to rethink and reinvent theater so that it does not disappear. This implies that theatrical performances have continued to be made by relying on communication channels and respecting restrictive measures. Television and social networks have been mechanisms through which theatre programs can be shown. Theatrical performances in strict compliance with restrictive measures and their dissemination on communication channels have helped to mitigate the death of the theater during the Covid-19 period. In addition, the themes portrayed in the performances have generally oriented toward prevention and the population's well-being. By multiplying theatrical performances during this difficult period and orienting the themes toward well-being, the actors ensure that the population's needs, values and priorities are at the heart of the recovery process. This adaptation shows that theater can be a means of social and psychological resilience in the face of crisis.

5.6. References

Azzopardi, F. (2020). Covid-19 en Afrique : quand confinement rime avec créativité artistique. *Revue Le point* [Online]. Available at: https://www.lepoint.fr/afrique [Accessed 04 October 2021].

Kamaté, A.B. (2020). L'Animation socioculturelle face à la pandémie de la Covid-19 en Côte d'Ivoire : synopsis d'une pratique en constante adaptation. In *Revues Echanges*, Volume 2. Université de Lomé.

N'gandu, P.N. (1993). *Théâtre et scène de spectacle : études sur les dramaturgies et les arts gestuels*. L'Harmattan, Paris.

Pavis, P. (2006). *Dictionnaire du théâtre*. Armand Colin, Paris.

Sameh, W., Ottone, E., Amirtahmasebi, R. (2020). La place de la culture dans la reprise post-Covid : un atout pour l'économie, la résilience et le bien-être. *Revue Opinion* [Online]. Available at: https://blogs.worldbank.org/fr [Accessed 4 October 2021].

Vandevelde, B. and Morhain, Y. (2012). Le groupe théâtre comme médiation thérapeutique auprès d'adolescents au processus de subjectivation entravé. *Psychothérapies*, 32(2), 125–135.

Oral sources

Interview with Koné Wagninlba Jocelyn, Artistic Director of Compagnie Nationale de Théâtre et de Danse au Centre National des Arts et de la Culture (CNAC), Côte d'Ivoire. 24 January 2022.

Interview with Ouattara Aminata, drama teacher at Institut National Supérieur des Arts et de l'Action Culturelle (INSAAC), Côte d'Ivoire. 21 January 2022.

Interview with Souleymane Sow, Ivorian stage director and drama teacher at Institut National Supérieur des Arts et de l'Action Culturelle (INSAAC), Côte d'Ivoire. 22 January 2022.

6

Tourism and the Pandemic: How to be Resilient and Creative Thanks to NICTs. Case study: Aloha Surf Camp in Morocco

Necessity is the mother of innovation[1]

Youssouf SOUMAHORO

Declared in January 2020 as a pandemic by the WHO, the Covid-19 has impacted most human activities. Tourism is one of the main sectors of the continent to suffer from this unprecedented situation. At the same time, the outlook in Africa looked promising according to the UNDP (the second fastest-growing tourism sector in the world).

This study aims to shed light on the resilience and creativity of certain tourism players in Morocco, who have used the health crisis as a springboard to diversify their offerings and clientele using Instagram. We evaluate how they adapted the face-to-face offering for local audiences, while offering virtual products to international audiences.

6.1. Introduction

According to the Moroccan Ministry of Tourism, Handicrafts and Social and Solidarity Economy, tourism "was among the sectors most affected by

---

Chapter written by Hanane MABROUK and John VAN DEN PLAS.

1 Expression used by Youssef during our in-depth interview about the resilience of his tourist accommodation. The original form of this proverb is: "necessity is the mother of invention". English expression taken from Gulliver's Travels by Swift.

the health crisis of 2020", causing a decrease in tourist arrivals of −79% in 2020 compared to 2019[2]. Berriane (2020) adds that tourism is "the only consumer product for which the consumer must travel to consume at the place of production [, and therefore] the sudden interruption of national and international traffic has resulted in a halt in activity". Despite the state's support to overcome this period of crisis (salary subsidies, deferral of tax payments), the event most awaited in 2021 by the incoming tourism sector in Morocco was the reopening of international borders in preparation for the summer season.

The tourism sector has experienced an unprecedented situation that has forced it to find urgent solutions to save the season. In this sense, Berriane (2020) says that "faced with this unprecedented crisis, the immediate solution is always the same: domestic tourism". Due to cancellations of international reservations, professionals are turning to domestic demand to save the season until better times return. However, a new intermediary has come into play in recent decades: new information and communication technologies (NICTs). The latter has enabled the actors of the sectors affected by the health crisis to reach new customers (digital and potentially real ones), despite the closure of borders.

In this chapter, we will report on a study conducted in 2021 (four weeks in January and six weeks in July–August) in one of Africa's most famous surfing tourist destinations: Taghazout Bay.

After a general portrait of the region and the research context, we will focus on the resilience of several local tourism actors by focusing on a more detailed study of an accommodation called Aloha Surf Camp. This Mecca of "surfing" tourism has reoriented its offering because of the innovative use of NICTs.

Finally, we will conclude by looking at the limits and perspectives of the research conducted by two partner laboratories: the communication laboratory LARLANCO of the University of Agadir Ibn Zohr and the Belgian multidisciplinary tourism laboratory.

---

2 Available at: https://mtataes.gov.ma/fr/tourisme/chiffres-cles-tourisme/indicateurs-du-secteur-touristique/ [Accessed on 30/10/2021].

6.2. Research methodology

The initial objective of this survey was to understand and identify the behaviors and places frequented by "digital nomads"[3], as observed in January 2021. However, as the field survey progresses by *"iteration"* (Olivier de Sardan 1997), that is, by going back and forth in a "non-linear way between informants and information", the object of the research gradually shifted to look at the way tourism professionals use NICTs to adapt to and survive the Covid-19 health crisis.

6.2.1. *Field surveys using ethnographic and sociological methods*

Data collection began in January 2021 (four weeks) and was completed in September 2021 (six weeks). The research area focused on the populations of the villages of Tamraght and Taghazout. Two researchers (one, a Belgian anthropologist specializing in tourism, and the other a Moroccan specialist in communication and digital technology) teamed up in this field study, which was conducted in two stages.

6.2.1.1. *Exploratory study in January 2021*

– Field study via a four-week immersion period in a surf camp in Tamraght allowing for "impregnation" and the collection of data[4] in Tamraght and Taghazout;

– first meetings with Ines Event, the Moroccan event company behind the first international surf show in Africa, the *Taghazout surf expo*[5];

– collaboration agreement between the Ulysse Lab-Network and the LARLANCO laboratory of the Ibn Zohr University of Agadir.

---

3 The concept of "digital nomad' will be defined in section 6.4.
4 As Olivier de Sardan (1997) reminds us, during immersion in the "field", the anthropologist records their observations and interactions so that they become "data and corpus". During the exploratory study, if these observations are not rigorously recorded, they allow for what he calls "impregnation".
5 This study is conducted within the framework of scientific days that will take place during this event initiated by this company in Agadir in January 2022.

6.2.1.2. *Participant observation in July and August 2021*

– Discussions in May with the different parties interested in the field studies (political actors, university and entrepreneurs);

– focus group with LARLANCO and Ulysse researchers;

– setting up the research team;

– participant observation in the surf and digital nomad community;

– observations[6], formal interviews and official data collection from local authorities[7].

To approach in a "direct way by slow and continuous impregnation" (Laplantine 2001, p. 17), while creating personalized links with the various actors of this field, the researchers lived in the center of Tamraght. In this way, they could share the daily lives of people living in or passing through this village over 10 weeks. The objective was to get into the "unconscious" and "underlying structure" (Lévi-Strauss 1974, p. 34) of the place and the local customs through this "intensive" fieldwork.

> Intensiveness also makes it possible to cross-check various sources of information constantly. It also makes it possible to link information because we work on a reduced scale, with in-depth knowledge of various orders and registers, to have a transversal, "holistic" approach (in the purely methodological sense of the term), where the social actors are apprehended in the diversity of their roles. (Olivier de Sardan 1997)

Jointly and individually, the researchers observed and conducted formal and informal interviews with tourism professionals (servers, managers) in Taghazout and Tamraght in August 2021 in French and Moroccan Darija (the vernacular language in Morocco).

---

6 Thiétart describes observation as "a mode of data collection by which the researcher observes, on his or her own, processes or behaviors taking place in an organization during a delimited period of time" (Thiétart et al. 2003, p. 238).

7 Olivier de Sardan (1997) indicates in this regard that "In the same social space, participant observation, in-depth interviews, survey techniques and the search for written documents are all stacked up", and therefore a prolonged period of time in the society being observed is the sine qua non of participant observation.

6.2.2. Research scope

The research (see Figure 6.1) was mainly conducted in the village of Tamraght (approximately 5,000 inhabitants), but several observations, participant observations, and interviews were also conducted in Taghazout (approximately 5,000 inhabitants). The objective was to spend most of the time with shopkeepers, servers, managers of cafés, restaurants, surf instructors, owners or managers of accommodation and national and international tourists.

Meetings, with varying levels of formality, were carried out with workers in luxury hotels in the Taghazout Bay, located along the recently constructed 4.5 km promenade between Taghazout village and Tamraght. The practice of surfing and skateboarding enabled the use of participant observation in the research area.

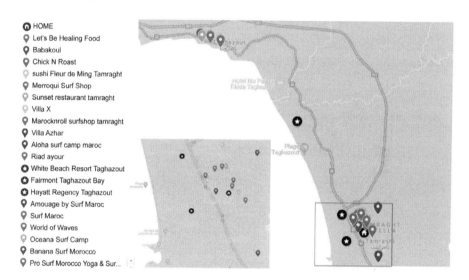

Figure 6.1. *Research area, with the hotel establishments visited[8] during this study. For a color version of this figure, see www.iste.co.uk/diallo/technologies.zip*

---

8 Each visit led to formal or less formal interviews that allowed us to triangulate information about the relationship between locals (from the villages of Taghazout and Tamraght) and tourists, but also between locals and Moroccans from other regions (or living abroad) who work in the two villages or spend their vacations there.

About 60 people were interviewed in formal and informal ways. These "informants"[9] were tourism and leisure professionals, foreigners (to the region, to the villages of Tamraght and Taghazout or non-Moroccans), tourists, but also non-tourism professional inhabitants (see Table 6.1).

Tourists (staying between 24 h and 3 months)		Tourism professionals, catering and coffee (even if not declared)		Non-professional residents		Other[10]	
Moroccans	Foreigners	Moroccans	Foreigners	Moroccans	Foreigners	Moroccans	Foreigners
6	7	13	6	5	2	9	8

Table 6.1. *Informant profiles*

Our approach centered on combining the accounts of our informants with official data, but also on "triangulation" between the divergent and convergent accounts, allowing us to identify the local social and economic context in detail, and understand how the tourist sector (and more precisely surf camps) experienced the health crisis caused by Covid-19.

6.3. Some geographical, economical and cultural notions of Moroccan surf tourism

If Morocco could be summed up in one word, there is no doubt that word would be diversity.[11]

Mohamed TEMSAMANI

Before getting to know the terrain, let's briefly return to the importance of tourism in Morocco economically, socially and culturally.

---

9 In anthropology, people interviewed formally and informally are referred to as such. Olivier de Sardan (1997) indicates that it is possible to distinguish several types of informants, especially among the so-called "privileged" informants: "Some are generalists, who give clear and easy access to the usual representations. Others are "smugglers", "mediators" or "gatekeepers", who open the way to other key actors or to cultural scenes that are difficult to access".

10 They could be researchers, digital nomads (those who are present more than three months a year), artists passing through or Moroccan entrepreneurs, Moroccans living abroad (MREs) or foreigners.

11 Quoted by Krastev (1999). Original publication: Temsamani M. (1997). *The Golden Book: Agadir and the Great South*. Bonechi, Italy.

6.3.1. *Tourism in Morocco*

Before the health crisis, tourism was the second largest contributor to the gross domestic product (GDP) and a creator of jobs, with 548,000 positions directly linked to economic activity. Agadir and Marrakech concentrated 62.6% of the demand, with large establishments capable of accommodating an average of 270 beds compared to 66 on average in the country (Berriane 2020). According to the Ministry of Tourism, Handicrafts and the Social and Solidarity Economy, "the travel restrictions adopted by the Moroccan government to limit the spread of the virus" have led to a decrease in tourist arrivals of 79% in 2020 compared to 2019, that is, 2.8 million tourists (non-residents). The impact on recorded tourist nights[12] has reduced them from 25.2 million in 2019 to 7 million in 2020 (–72%), with a decrease in travel revenues of –54%.[13]

6.3.2. *The Bay of Taghazout: a flagship destination for "surf" and "luxury" tourism*

The Moroccan coastline has seen the emergence of surfing since the 1960s. For a long time, surfing was associated with hippies, outsiders and a bohemian lifestyle of "wild" camping and fireside parties. Taghazout (located 23 km north of Agadir) has even become the Mecca of this new leisure activity, which began in the 1970s on its shores with the arrival of the first Australian and American tourists (Berriane and Moizo 2021). At that time, the village of Taghazout did not even officially exist and was mainly composed of a few shacks for fishermen.

"It was built later by people who came down from the mountains without the authorities knowing about it"[14], says a 63-year-old Taghazout native and former hippie.

This discourse corroborates recent research on the region, indicating that

> Taghazout was originally a village created by peasant-fishermen who came down there seasonally from their mountainous lands

---

12 Within the limits of this survey, we will discuss the figures that are difficult to establish because the tourism sector, and more specifically accommodation, is difficult to quantify.
13 Available at: https://mtataes.gov.ma/fr/tourisme/chiffres-cles-tourisme/indicateurs-du-secteur-touristique/ [Accessed 30 October 2021].
14 Excerpt from an interview in August 2021.

and villages of the Western High Atlas. Living on agriculture and sedentary livestock in difficult conditions, these peasants moved to the coast during the fishing seasons in search of supplements provided by a sea full of fish. They built a few shacks that served as seasonal lodgings and storage places, which gave rise to the initial nucleus of the present village (Ibid.).

From the 1970s, Agadir, like many coastal cities whose local economy is suffering, turned to mass seaside tourism. However, Taghazout was first visited by "hippies" and even some famous personalities of this movement, like Jimi Hendrix and Frank Zappa, during the 1970s (Ibid.). Later, in the 1990s, tourists in search of waves suitable for surfing (first foreigners, and then recently Moroccans) began to regularly visit the village, which is now known worldwide for the quality and diversity of its surfing spots.

In the 2000s, this coastal area was described as "devoid of urbanization" or, with a still "wild" charm in travel guides such as the Routard, which naturally attracted European tourists seeking to escape the winters of the North. The latter established "wilderness campsites" on parking lots or dotted dunes, with argan trees seen at sea for several months (Ibid.).

Today, Taghazout and its bay (including the village of Tamraght) are still known for its waves, with dozens of stores specializing in surfing and surf camps, and since 2020, for its brand new 5-star hotel complexes forming the Taghazout Bay project. Despite the construction of these new hotels that increase the capacity to 12,000 beds, this tourist area is appreciated by tourists for its "warm welcome", "authenticity" and "charm".

6.3.3. *Cultural diversity*

Foreign tourists are now joined by Moroccan tourists who describe these beaches as "cleaner" than other seaside resorts, but also more "open" in terms of "mentality". According to several informants, the reason for this "open-mindedness" is linked to the contacts established for decades between locals and Western tourists ("hippies" and then "surfers"), giving this Moroccan coast a "unique" atmosphere, with a mixture of tradition and modernity.

We may also add the Moroccan cultural diversity between the Gadiris (inhabitants of the city of Agadir), the Chleuh (inhabitants originating from the villages of Taghazout and Tamraght, who speak the Berber dialect

Tachelhit) and other regions of Morocco represented across workers in the tourist sector. These different profiles can be a source of conflict or misunderstanding[15], but also of cultural connection (Jean-Loup 2001), reinforcing a multiculturalism "characterized by a back-and-forth between Arab-Berber-Islamic tradition" (Moha 2009) and more Western customs. According to Guibert and Arab (2016), "surfing can be positioned at the intersection of a 'Western' type of sporting activity on the one hand, and 'traditional' signifiers on the other. The presence of markers and the arrangement of objects – objectified and crystallized social – allow for the exposure of the ambivalence of surfing images".

6.3.4. *Surf camps*

With nearly 80 km of coastline and more than 50 "spots" (places suitable for surfing) suitable for both beginners and advanced surfers, Taghazout Bay and its surroundings "allow surfing in all seasons [relying] on local knowledge about the conditions of the marine environment, representations acquired across generations of local fishermen, to which most of the chaperones, guides and speakers in surf schools belong" (Berriane and Moizo 2021). Guibert and Arab (2016) indicate that Taghazout and Agadir have about 15 stores that specialize in surfing, and about 40 *surf camps*, which they define as "dwellings fitted out to accommodate international surfers" (Ibid.).

According to our observations in the field, it is important to qualify this definition while questioning their number and adding different categories of surf camps.

Over time, the clientele has diversified from the "hippies" of the 1970s to families (foreign or Moroccan) or business tourists and digital nomads wanting to take advantage of the place to practice a board sport[16] while

---

15 Many of the qualified profiles in the field of tourism come from other regions and do not speak the endemic language (Tachelhit), which sometimes makes it difficult to collaborate and hire staff from both villages.

16 In addition to surfing, other board sports have developed in recent years, such as stand up paddle (a longboard on which the practitioner moves forward in a standing position because of an oar), bodyboarding (practiced with flippers in a prone position, with the upper half of the body on a board smaller than the surfboards) or bodysurfing (the practitioner uses their body as a "board" to catch the waves).

working. Each of these categories has created distinct offerings that can be described as follows:

– "roots" surf camps: hippie atmosphere (alcohol and marijuana), group meals (and participation), shared rooms or dormitories;

– "luxury" surf camps: accommodation adapted to groups, families and couples, with a service in double rooms, triple rooms or high-end apartments.

Both types of accommodation are usually chosen for surfing and include surfing lessons (usually twice a day) and group or individual sightseeing trips in the area.

It is important to note that for several years, Moroccan tourists have been visiting these places, which were initially designed for Westerners but are increasingly popular with the inhabitants of large Moroccan cities, whether in groups of friends or families.

Second, mixed categories between the gite and the vacation apartment are often present on online booking sites such as Airbnb or Booking.com. These places can be chosen for vacations, with or without surfing, and allow groups of friends[17] or families to enjoy a space dedicated to them. Surfboards are available, and accommodation managers can offer services ranging from meals to cultural or surfing excursions. Price ranges vary depending on the comfort and services required.

Lastly, we must mention the hotels of varying degrees of luxury offering surf lessons with Moroccan instructors to their customers.

Quantifying the surf camps or accommodations offering surfing lessons or equipment is difficult because most are not officially listed and are known only through word of mouth and specialized online booking sites such as Booking.com, Tripadvisor or simply via Google Maps. Officially, about 70 accommodations (figures from January 2020) offering services around surfing (boards and courses) are known by the authorities of Aourir (Tamraght) and Taghazout, and about 50 of them are authorized (the others are in the process of authorization or must close).

---

17 This type of accommodation is also often chosen to circumvent the law prohibiting an unmarried couple or friends of opposite sexes from staying outside their respective addresses.

According to local surf operators, there were more than 150 surf camps before the health crisis, half of which closed during the lockdown.

6.4. Conceptual framework

The case of Aloha Surf Camp Maroc that we analyze next requires us to understand several conceptual elements that we explore below.

6.4.1. *Tourism and social networks*

Although sharing information and opinions have always existed, digital social networks have amplified the phenomenon while expanding the size of the audience.

For the past 15 years, tourism professionals have been using new technologies to connect consumers with their products before they travel to inform them and make them want to visit the tourist destination (via Facebook and, more recently, Instagram, TripAdvisor, YouTube or even TikTok). Social networks promote the development of what Millerand et al. (2010) call "participatory cultures" and "contributory cultures". For more than a decade, digital platforms have become real "mediums"[18], that is to say, "an ecosystem in which humans act, interact, evolve, and live" (Atchoua et al. 2020), their future, current, and past tourism experience.

Considered a means of expression, especially because of the dissemination of opinions (Godes and Mayzlin 2004), and also because of its hedonic value (Holbrook and Hirschman 1982), using social media has more impact when attracting the attention of travelers to use content proposed on social networks to plan their trips. On the other hand, those who defend a more qualitative approach (Kozinets 2020), which was inherited from the anthropological tradition, and influenced by the work of Manchester School in the 1950s–1960s, show an interest in networks that are posed as specific objects (Eve 2002). This latter approach allows for a better account of individual behavior within the social network studied (Mercklé 2004). Social networks are central to the strategy of "experiential" tourism, which is based

---

18 Concept evoked by Bachimont (2015).

on a personalized relationship with the client (almost intimate) and the individualization of services. The network creates a real "community" that shares experiences, emotions and sensations. Consuming the service is not simply functional, but reveals it is symbolic, hedonic, or aesthetic. The tourist becomes a "consum'actor" (Raffour 2010), a partner who not only participates in the promotion of services by recommending them, but also shares their emotions. Social media also allows a certain engagement to provide personalized information to each customer. Managers need to tailor the content (service) to each visitor's situation (Zeng and Gerritsen 2014). Social networks offer practical and useful knowledge of the "client-tourist" for the strategy to be carried out more interactively (Berriane 2020). The offer is co-constructed, with this customer, creative, and collaborative, through this "back and forth". The tourism service seizes this opportunity for co-creation.

Value creation is done through interaction with and by the customer (Lusch et al. 2007). In other words, the digital revolution has profoundly transformed consumer behavior through access to information. The place of the tourist-customer and their role in the commercial relationship have been redefined; new modes of consumption are emerging, such as "collaborative" consumption. On the one hand, "the user no longer needs to have in-depth knowledge of computers" (Pélissier and Qotb 2012). On the other hand, the democratization of usage allows each Internet user to be both a reader and a contributor. Communication becomes transversal and takes the form of tags, opinions or comments (Auray 2020).

6.4.2. *Digital nomadism*

A "digital nomad" is a person who, through the ability to work remotely via a computer, can work from anywhere in the world when connected to the Internet. The term "digital nomad" comes from an eponymous book published two decades ago by electrical engineers Tsugio Makimoto and David Manners (1998). Digital nomadism referred to "traveling technology workers who create websites, run online businesses, develop mobile applications, and design online marketing resources, but also to artists, graphic designers, videographers, and craftspeople". Other profiles called "nomadic capitalists", that is, "owners of successful businesses based on online platforms that they manage while traveling permanently or regularly", have emerged in recent years.[19] The number of people adopting this "lifestyle"[20] is increasing year after year. The pandemic has favored this practice (sometimes becoming the only solution to reduce cases of this phenomenon spreading). New professions have been added to the profiles described above, with professions that were once far removed from the digital world, but that Covid 19 has switched to remote work (teachers, secretaries, project coordinators). This travel-to-work trend offers new possibilities for the more traditional hotel sector, as seen in the following points.

The Figure 6.2 represents the increase in searches for this concept on Google during the health crisis.

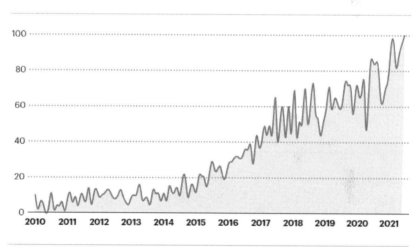

Figure 6.2. *Popularity of the term "digital nomad" (as a percentage of current numbers)*[21]

---

19 Available at: https://fr.forumviesmobiles.org/projet/2020/08/01/nomades-numeriques-lere-covid-19-13408 (Laura Stanik and Maurie Cohen, 2020).

20 We have borrowed this term from the sociologist Luca Patarroni, who refers to a "way of life" as a composition – in time and space – of daily activities and experiences that give meaning and shape to the life of a person or group.

21 Available at: https://www.ledevoir.com/economie/617877/travail-les-nomades-numeriques-surfer-sur-la-vague-du-teletravail.

6.5. Results and discussions

6.5.1. *Case study: Aloha surf camp*

As mentioned above, the first contact with this well-known surf camp in the village of Tamraght was initiated following our research into places that could accommodate digital nomads. After several visits, informal interviews, and an overnight stay, this surf camp emerged as the most interesting case regarding resilience and adaptation to the village's Covid crisis.

For the next few points, we base ourselves on an in-depth interview with Youssef Alouam (manager of the surf camp) and our participant observation (those who stayed several nights on site). We call him Joe, his alternative name. At the age of 26, he has solid experience in different sectors and wears several hats: surfer, manager of Aloha, musician, DJ and music producer. He trained in music production (in Turkey) and the hotel business to manage his father's surf camp (Aloha Surf Camp) and develop it internationally. Several trips to Brazil and Indonesia allowed him to test several types of accommodation and tourism practices (including digital nomadism, which he includes in his later projects).

6.5.2. *The surf camp*

Joe's father, Abedssamade El Aouam, created the surf camp in the early 2000s to meet a demand that has been very present in the region since the 1990s. He was a surfer and had a background in construction and music.

The facility is perched on the heights of Tamraght. It has a large building divided into several parts: the common area, a low accommodation part and a high one (see illustration below). The structure can accommodate about 50 people. Above the common area is a room dedicated to yoga outside (on the parking lot), and a large ramp (half-pipe) can be used for skateboarding.

The services generally include surfing courses, yoga classes and excursions in the tourist areas around the village (or even in the middle of the country).

In the common area, a pool table, the reception, a large table for 10 people, a lounge, and some frames dedicated to surfing and local culture. Some boards, with some charters of benevolence in the best, and stickers "Calmness", "The ceiling [...] not the limit", The view [...]. There is also a bar, with a buffet, and a large bay window overlooking the terrace overlooking the spots of Banana, Devils rock, and the Taghazout bay resort[22].

Photo: Facebook page of Aloha Surf Camp Maroc. For a color version of this photo, see www.iste.co.uk/diallo/technologies.zip

The clientele mainly visits to do week-long surfing courses, and the marketing tools used were sites like Tripadvisor, Facebook and Instagram since 2015.
The images shared on these two networks mostly depicted surfing, beaches or yoga (like most other surf camps in the area).
Image: Instagram account alohasurcampmaroc, which has 13,000 followers. For a color version of this photo, see www.iste.co.uk/diallo/technologies.zip

22 Excerpt from John Van Den Plas' field notebook.

In 2016, the surf camp space evolved following Joe's international experiences in Brazil and Indonesia as part of a project between Aloha Surf Camp, a Brazilian campsite, and Aloha Bali in Indonesia.[23] Joe gradually adapted his hosting to digital nomadism as a result of his travels and also his Master's degree in digital marketing, which he received in 2017. He said the "surf" atmosphere was potentially compatible with the digital nomad audience. He indicates that the only requirement is to have "a good internet connection, and a homogeneous group [...]. From there, the coworking activity is very easy to set up".

Because of Instagram, Joe has attracted many digital nomads looking for places suitable for coworking while having a healthy lifestyle, a good connection and a good atmosphere.

6.5.3. *Crisis management: between resilience and innovation*

Few tourists (surfers or digital nomads) stayed in Morocco when the borders closed. This moment at the pandemic's peak gave Joe much time to reflect and get closer to a passion other than surfing: music. Self-taught, he gained experience as a DJ and amateur guitarist by rehearsing in his room, then in a small studio he set up in the surf camp, allowing him to build relationships with local artists. He invited Moroccan artists for mini concerts or jam sessions in the surf camp, gradually transforming the space designed for the surfing apprentices. Via word of mouth (and especially through Instagram), his new project Aloha Vibes quickly took on an unexpected scale, with videos being seen thousands of times and more than 10,000 subscribers in a few months.

6.5.4. *From surfing tourists to nomadic artists*

Today, Aloha Vibes offers artistic residencies and studio recordings in an environment conducive to creativity and inspiration. Surrounded by a multidisciplinary team (beatmaker, musicians, art director and digital communication specialists), it also allows artists to conceptualize and record tracks, taking advantage of the visibility of its social networks (Aloha Surf Camp and Aloha Vibes). The most innovative part is probably the idea named Aloha Live. These are live online concerts broadcasted via YouTube

---

23 He worked in particular on the adaptation of places for digital nomads.

featuring well-known artists remixing their music with an instrumental band. These videos have been viewed hundreds of thousands to millions of times on YouTube, and the Instagram page created on September 13, 2020, already has 11,000 followers.

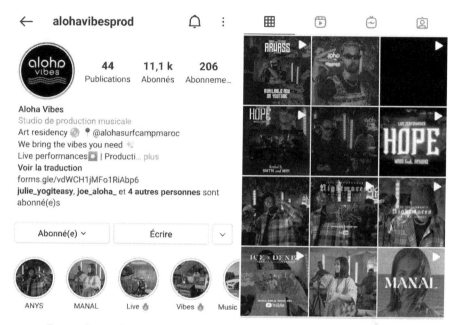

For a color version of this photo, see www.iste.co.uk/diallo/technologies.zip

6.5.5. *Perspectives for "Aloha" projects*

While the world went through an unprecedented health crisis caused by the Covid-19 pandemic, all eyes turned toward the future. For Joe, combining his father Abedssamad El Aouam's experience and his own is an asset that has allowed him to define a niche between accommodation, surfing, artistic activities and coworking.

Thanks to new technologies, including Instagram, Joe's dream (of working in music) is becoming a reality, and the obstacles (a forced transition to digital) have turned into advantages. Aloha Surf camp is now known worldwide for surfing, digital nomadism and music. For Joe, the three audiences (surfers, digital nomads and artists in residence) are compatible (sometimes complementary) and allow the surf camp to have a minimum fill rate during the year, even in a new crisis.

The recording studio is also an attractive feature, as it is one of the only studios in the Taghazout region, and it now attracts artists from other countries, especially Europe. Joe's next goal is to create an ALOHA label, while developing his current activities with partners worldwide. Surfing has put Tamraght and Taghazout on the map of surfing sports, and maybe this studio will give new life to this region[24].

6.6. Conclusion

The health crisis has revealed the flaws and structural constraints from which the sector suffers. The post-Covid era must be an opportunity to review the current tourism model to make it a vector for national development. Efforts must be made to ensure better industry governance, accelerate digital transformation and enable resilience in future crises.

In this case study, we illustrated how a tourism player took advantage of the crisis as an opportunity to transform its core business using multiple ICTs.

This research has limitations that appear as future issues to be explored. For example, since not all establishments are officially registered, obtaining representative figures for tourist activity is difficult. The same is true for the number of tourists, which is almost impossible to count because the data are based on "only foreign visitors entering the country, and therefore it does not include the arrivals of Moroccans living abroad" (Berriane 2020). Our qualitative methodological choices via ethnographic (participant observation) and micro-sociological methods do not allow us to generalize our results to all tourism organizations. However, they allow us to document the innovative practices of tourism professionals, whom some authors sometimes consider uncreative or even outdated with the new trends in the sector (Berriane 2020).

---

24 Other places for digital nomads and artistic residences are currently being created in the village, mainly because of the publicity created by Aloha, but also due to the recording possibilities of their studio.

6.7. References

Alzouma, G. (2009). Téléphone mobile, Internet et développement : l'Afrique dans la société de l'information ? *Société de l'information*, 2(2) [Online]. Available at: http://journals.openedition.org/ticetsociete/488 [Accessed 31 October 2021].

Atchoua, J., Bogui, J.-J., Diallo, S. (2020). *Digital Technologies and African Societies: Challenges and Opportunities*. ISTE Ltd., London and John Wiley & Sons, New York.

Bachimont, B. (2017). Le numérique comme milieu : enjeux épistémologiques et phénoménologiques : principes pour une science des données. *Interfaces numériques*, 4(3), 402–402.

Berriane, M. (2020). Le tourisme marocain de l'après Covid 19. *Téoros* [Online]. Available at: http://journals.openedition.org/teoros/7627 [Accessed 30 September 2021].

Berriane, M. and Moizo, B. (2020). De la barque à la planche, de la planche au béton : changements et adaptations liés au tourisme à Taghazout (littoral Atlantique, Maroc). In *Les mondes du surf : transformations historiques, trajectoires sociales, bifurcations technologiques*, Guibert, C. (ed.). Maison des Sciences de l'Homme d'Aquitaine.

Doueihi, M. (2011). *Pour un humanisme numérique*. Le Seuil, Paris.

El Bouhali, B.S. (2020). Covid-19 au Maroc, un "choc" de tourisme intérieur est indispensable. *L'Economiste* [Online]. Available at: https://www.leconomiste.com/article/1061160-covid-19-au-maroc-un-choc-de-tourisme-interieur-est-indispensable [Accessed 24 August 2021].

Guibert, C. and Arab, C. (2016). Être surfeuse au Maroc : les conditions d'une socialisation à contre-courant. *Terrains & Travaux*, 28, 175–198 [Online]. Available at: https://www.cairn.info/revue-terrains-et-travaux-2016-1-page-175.htm [Accessed 30 September 2021].

Jean-Loup, A. (2001). *Branchements. Anthropologie de l'universalité des cultures*. Flammarion, Paris.

Krastev, A. (1999). Le Surf Au Maroc un potentiel plein d'avenir. Thesis, Institut Supérieur International du Tourisme Au Maroc, Morocco.

Laplantine, F. (2001). *L'Anthropologie*. Bibliothèque Payot, Paris.

Lévi-Strauss, C. (1974). *Anthropologie Structurale*. Plon, Paris.

Najat, R. (2020). Surveillance technologies in the Covid-19 era. *Policy Centre* [Online]. Available at: https://www.policycenter.ma/sites/default/files/2021-01/PB-20-57Redouan_Najah_EN.pdf [Accessed 30 September 2021].

OECD (2021). La transformation numérique à l'ère du covid 19. Renforcer la résilience et combler les facteurs. Supplément à l'édition 2020 des perspectives de l'économie numérique [Online]. Available at: www.oecd.org/fr/numerique/transformation-numerique-covid.pdf [Accessed 30 September 2021].

Olivier de Sardan, J.-P. (1997). La politique du terrain. *Enquête*, 1, 71–109 [Online]. Available at: http://journals.openedition.org/enquete/263 [Accessed October 29 2021].

PNUD (2021). Maximiser la contribution du tourisme à la reprise post-Covid-19 en Afrique. Press release [Online]. Available at: https://www1.undp.org/content/undp/fr/home/news-centre/news/2021/maximiser-la-contribution-du-tourisme-a-la-reprise-post-covid-19.html [Accessed 30 September 2021].

Thietard, R.-A. (2003). *Méthodes de recherche en management*. Dunod, Paris.

PART 3

Business, Education and Covid

7

Digital Technologies to Support Learning in the University Environment During the Pandemic at UFHB: From Hope to Disillusionment

Integrating Information and Communication Technologies (ICT) in higher education in Africa is new. The COVID 19 pandemic had a significant effect on education in Africa. Many educational institutions were closed to help stop the spread of the virus. Instead, many educational providers offered online training and collaborative work through platforms such as *Zoom, Blackboard* and *Teams*. The use of e-learning through collaborative work and telework platforms such as Zoom, Blackboard, Teams was quickly identified by decision makers as a viable solution and a real opportunity to successfully integrate these tools into the education system of many African countries. This study, through a qualitative survey (*focus groups*) conducted with 44 students (from students doing Bachelor degrees to Master's) of the Department of Information and Communication Sciences (DSIC) at the University Félix Houphouët-Boigny (UFHB) in Abidjan, focuses on the experience of virtual learning which was initiated in this department in 2020. The results of this study show us how this experience was welcomed with great hope but, due to various factors, turned out to be a great disappointment.

7.1. Introduction

In an article published in 2008, Djénéba Traoré ponders the future of the pedagogical use of digital technologies in sub-Saharan Africa. She considers

---

Chapter written by Jean-Jacques Maomra BOGUI.

that "the integration of ICTs is becoming an unavoidable phenomenon, particularly in the education sector, where their use seems to be able to promote access to information, facilitate the construction of knowledge and the acquisition of skills, as well as increase the educational success and employability of young people". According to her, digital technologies are powerful cognitive tools that allow young Africans to access "new opportunities for openness and learning". However, their use in education "deserves to be studied by African researchers in the specific contexts of the continent to inform ongoing policy dialogues and ICT integration processes".

Over the last few decades, many studies have focused on implementing digital technologies in African education systems. A large number of African and non-African researchers are interested in the issue of integration. The use of ICTs in education in Africa (Blé 2001; Ducasse 2002; Bahi 2004, 2006, 2008; Karsenti and Ngamo 2007; Bogui, 2008; Traoré 2008; Mian 2010) has provided us with a relatively rich and relevant literature on this subject. Most of these studies emphasize the difficulties in implementing policies to integrate ICT into education. The issue of access to ICT and the pedagogical use of these tools is still a major concern.

A study entitled *Enquête sur les TICS en éducation en Afrique* conducted by the *Programme Information pour le Développement* (infoDev) published in 2007 states that ICT policies in African countries act as a catalyst for the development of ICT policies in education. According to the study's authors, most ICT policies for the education sector have been developed since 2000 in most African countries. The report shows that developing an ICT policy for education is a long and complex process. However, most ICT/education policies in Africa are very comprehensive (in that they include all sectors of the education system). The report also notes that ICT/education policies in Africa emphasize the need to improve access to digital technologies by key stakeholders in the education system. The very important role played by donors (UNECA, USAID, UNDP, AfDB, IDRC) in the policy process is also highlighted. However, difficulties in the implementation of ICT/education plans are conveyed. Indeed, while ICT/education policies articulate a vision, implementation plans focus on practical aspects needed to achieve this vision. This report highlights African universities' enormous difficulties in accessing or renewing infrastructure and equipment and integrating ICT into university pedagogy.

7.2. Digital technologies to support training in the university environment

Indeed, according to some experts, the integration of digital technologies should allow the quality of higher education in Africa to evolve and lead African universities to adopt more active pedagogy focused on the learner and their learning. Understanding the skills that need to be developed in the school of the 21st century appears to be a challenge for all actors in the education system (Moura et al. 2008). In the knowledge society, curricula stop prescribing what teachers should teach and instead indicate what students should learn. Adopting this new paradigm helps rethink education to meet the demands of today's society. As Bryan Alexander (2004) claims, it is a matter of "inviting students to move from being passive consumers to being creative and communicative participants". To achieve this, the teacher must accept that they are no longer to take on the role of a knowledge disseminator (Harvey 2002). They must stop being the one who provides solutions and become a facilitator, helping students to find relevant information and build their knowledge. This change in the vision of pedagogy in the digital age thus challenges many African researchers in the field of education.

Among the works surrounding the issue carried out by African researchers, we can cite the study by Mian Bi (2010) on ICT and education in Côte d'Ivoire in which the author shows that "ICT was initially inaccessible, then accessible, but playful, and finally it seems to be increasingly used as a tool for quality education and training". The author of this study considers that the integration of ICTs in the African education system is responding to the need to correct the deficiencies from which it suffers. Indeed, according to Mian Bi, "one of the major educational challenges of African countries is to improve the rate of schooling and the quality of teaching". One of the main advantages of this ICT integration for several authors is African learners' access to educational resources via the Internet.

In an article published in 2008, Aghi and Gadou (2008), through the results of qualitative research conducted at the UFHB in Abidjan with various actors in higher education (19 teacher-researchers, 12 doctoral students and seven members of the administrative and technical staff), are interested in the power issues related to the predominance of the Internet in the Ivorian university field. According to these authors, personal ambition and power dynamics structure the university field's logic, which does not favor establishing a space for scientific debate through the Internet (Bahi and Gadou 2008).

Zacharia Tiemtoré (2007) shows that "the integration of ICT in education, with the declared objective to resolve structural, institutional and pedagogical difficulties and to catch up with the industrialized countries on a socioeconomic level, constitutes a utopia at the current stage of development in Burkina Faso, a utopia based on a mythical interpretation of technologies".

7.3. Difficulties when appropriating ICTs within academic institutions in Africa

However, although the field of higher education and research is one of the pioneers in the integration of digital technologies in French-speaking Africa, mainly because of the initiatives of French language scientific cooperation organizations such as the *Institut de recherche pour le développement* (IRD) and the *Agence Universitaire de la Francophonie* (Ducasse 2002), the lack of take up of these technologies by local actors (teacher-researchers, students and administrators) has been a major obstacle to the successful integration of these technologies in academic institutions for several decades. With this in mind, in 2011, an agreement was signed in Paris between the WAEMU Commission[1] and UNESCO[2] for the implementation of a project to support universities in the WAEMU region to integrate digital technologies that can help implement the Bachelor's–Master's–Doctorate (BMD) system, which is one of the major reforms of the higher education system in countries belonging to this regional organization.

Promoting the take up of ICTs by actors in university institutions in the WAEMU region is a real challenge for the initiators of the PADTICE

---

1 West African Monetary Union.
2 United Nations Educational, Scientific and Cultural Organization.

project. Indeed, the issue of the integration and use of digital technologies in university education in Africa is not a new concern. Since the 1960s, each decade has witnessed the experimentation of programs aimed at transferring media technologies (videotex, audio and video conferencing, digital campuses) trending in universities throughout Western countries and African universities, with varying degrees of success. Most of the time, these programs did not get to the end of the pilot project, and a level of disengagement was seen within international organizations at the origin of these projects. The very low level of involvement of the main local actors (students, teachers, administrative staff) in the design and implementation of these projects partly explains the difficulties these projects face, which are rarely inspired by existing practices in the African university environment. The only expectation is that local actors will adopt the proposed innovation.

Although it is most often problems of means and infrastructure that are generally cited by actors, and more particularly teacher-researchers, to justify the failure of most of the programs set up since the 1960s to allow the integration of digital technologies in the African university environment, some researchers consider that the very low involvement of African higher education actors in these programs is certainly one of the main causes of their failure (Tahiri-Leborgne 2002). Indeed, the lack of appropriation of these technologies from the West by university actors in Africa (teachers, researchers or administrators) generally results in a very low level of participation by the latter in these different programs, which are most often set up within the framework of cooperation with countries in the North or on the initiative of international organizations working in the field of development (Ducasse 2002). Higher education actors in Africa are often satisfied with limited participation in these initiatives initiated by Western institutions. In the era adopting the BMD system in French-speaking West Africa, the successful appropriation of digital technologies by higher education actors in Côte d'Ivoire and their integration into university pedagogy can be seen as one of the greatest challenges of the moment for the higher education system in this country.

7.4. Improved access to ICTs, the digital divide in secondary education

While it is easy to see that access to ICTs has improved significantly, mainly because of the personal initiatives of teacher-researchers and students, skills needed to use the tools for pedagogy and university learning are still very uneven. Indeed, even with a certain democratization of access to laptops for teachers-researchers and smartphones for students, we can note that the digital divide concerning access to technological equipment, greatly criticized about two decades ago, is beginning to be resolved. Yet, another digital divide called the "second degree" digital divide can be uncovered today. In this regard, it can be noted that for several years now, several researchers have been looking into this issue of the "second degree" digital divide (DiMaggio and Hargittai 2002).

For these researchers, beyond the issues related to inequalities in access to ICTs, it is rather a question of inequality in the effective use of these tools that are at the center of their concerns (Rallet and Rochelandet 2004). Camacho (2005) has written about digital divides, saying that they "result from the possibilities or difficulties for social groups to take advantage, collectively, of information and communication technologies to transform the reality in which they evolve and to improve the living conditions of their members". Thus, for Brotcorne and Valenduc (2009), the question of users' digital skills becomes central. They distinguish three levels of digital skills: instrumental skills (technical and reasoning skills in the face of technological hazards), informational skills (the ability to search for, select, understand and evaluate information) and strategic skills (the ability to make sense of information in one's life and to make decisions that may have implications for one's professional or personal environment) (Brotcorne and Valenduc 2009).

As Camacho (2005) points out, as with other populations, rather than issues of access, issues of use and quality of use are driving the growing digital divide.

7.5. The Covid-19 pandemic as a catalyst for the integration of ICTs into pedagogy and learning in the university setting

Since December 2019, the whole world has suffered the effects of a health crisis with particularly worrying consequences. It is from China, more precisely from the city of Wuhan (capital of Hubei in central China), that a new viral disease caused by an unknown coronavirus has spread rapidly across the planet, leading to it being declared a global pandemic by the World Health Organization (WHO) in March 2020, under the name Covid-19 for "coronavirus disease 2019".

Faced with this threat which has had tragic and devastating consequences for the economic and social development of states, governments worldwide declared a state of emergency and took a series of restrictive measures to reduce the speed at which the virus spread. Populations saw their daily lives disrupted with the adoption of extraordinary measures such as physical or social distancing, establishing a physical distance of at least 1 m between individuals, the mandatory wearing of masks, the prohibition or temporary reduction of travel and curfews.

Côte d'Ivoire was not exempt from this and implemented its response plan to this pandemic. Since the identification of the first case of infection in the country on March 11, 2021, the disease has continued to evolve in successive waves while remaining less noteworthy compared to what was observed on other continents. However, it has affected economic, social and cultural life and the nation's morale. Among the precautionary measures taken by the Ivorian government at the beginning of the crisis to avoid the virus spreading, we can note the decision to close all schools and universities for 2 months in the first semester of 2020. Following the example of many other countries, the Ivorian government and the heads of these institutions identified Information and Communication Technologies for Education (ICTEs) as an appropriate solution to continue training Ivorian pupils and students in compliance with the barriers. It should be recognized that virtual learning or online courses are increasingly practiced throughout the world. The Covid-19 pandemic has amplified the phenomenon insofar as the implementation of generalized virtual learning in Côte d'Ivoire has been favored by the outbreak of the Covid-19 pandemic.

Thus, at the University Félix Houphouët-Boigny of Cocody in Abidjan, the oldest and largest university (by the number of registered students and Training and Research Units) in Côte d'Ivoire, the university council tried to "save" the 2020–2021 academic year. The University Félix Houphouët-Boigny, like many academic institutions around the world, tried to implement a virtual learning system with the recommendation to all departments to use the collaborative communication and teleworking platform Microsoft Teams for university teaching.

In the framework of our study, we are interested in the experience carried out in this sense at the Department of Information and Communication Sciences (DSIC) of the University Félix Houphouët-Boigny.

Implementing these online courses for DSIC was achieved within constraints that need to be explored. Indeed, in a university environment where free access to rooms equipped with computers and a high-speed Internet connection is a real privilege, as is access to a Wi-Fi network on the university campus and the possession of a personal computer by students, such an initiative appears to be a particularly bold challenge.

However, the high penetration of cell phones in Africa can be seen through the consumption of this technological tool by young Ivorians, particularly students in information and communication sciences at the University of Félix Houphouët-Boigny. Thus, the cell phone (smartphone), a popular tool, quickly appeared as a significant alternative to fill the technological deficits mentioned above to allow students to follow these courses virtually.

Given the singularity of the context in which this experiment in online training is taking place, we are legitimately entitled to ask ourselves several questions:

– How do UFHB DSIC students perceive online training in the Ivorian university training environment?

– How do UFHB DSIC students take online courses from their cell phones?

This research aims to analyze DSIC students' perceptions of the online learning experience at UFHB and to describe their use of cell phones in implementing online courses.

7.6. Methodology: meeting the students

The exploratory research we conducted with UFHB DSIC students is essentially qualitative, and it was conducted in April 2021 using a focus group discussion guide. The focus group interviews on the UFHB campus lasted between 60 and 80 min on average. We interviewed 44 DSIC students (17 girls and 27 boys) whose levels ranged from a Bachelor's degree to a Master's degree in information and communication sciences. It seems appropriate to emphasize that the students of the DSIC begin the specialization in the 3rd year of their undergraduate degree (License III). Thus, this department offers four courses: journalism, political and organizational communication, advertising marketing, and finally, communication for development.

During the focus group interviews, we asked students about their use of cell phones, their perception of online learning, their opinion of online pedagogy at DSIC, their experience with online courses and their criticisms and suggestions on the issue. Interviews with five focus groups of 7 to 10 students were conducted during this period.

7.7. Focus group characteristics

Each of the interview groups consisted of the following:

– In Master II, the group comprised three girls and five boys. The specialties represented were advertising-marketing, development communication and political and organizational communication.

– In Master I, the group was composed of three girls and four boys, and the specialties represented were advertising-marketing, development communication and political and organizational communication.

– In License III, we interviewed one group of four girls and six boys from the political and organizational communication course, and another group of License III students composed of three girls and six boys from the advertising-marketing and development communication specialties.

– Finally, in License II, the interview group was composed of four girls and six boys.

7.8. Smartphones, the students' tool of choice

Our investigations revealed that all of the students interviewed during our group interview sessions owned a smartphone. As a rule, their phone was mainly used for the following activities:

– staying in touch with their loved ones (calls, SMS);

– entertaining (listening to music, going on social networks);

– doing Google searches related to their studies.

The average time the students used a smartphone was between 3 and 5 years. They unanimously affirmed that the cell phone occupied an important place in their study because it was their main tool (for research, following online courses, and tutorial group work).

7.9. UFHB students' perception of online learning

According to the information collected, students claimed they had only been doing online courses for 2 years (WhatsApp for the 2019–2020 academic year and Microsoft Teams for the 2020–2021 academic year).

They considered that conditions were not met for taking online courses in Côte d'Ivoire. The reasons for this were the unpreparedness, the lack of prior training of the actors (students, teachers, and administrative and technical staff), the unavailability of an Internet connection in several places on campus and the absence of a Wi-Fi network on the university domain.

Students' main reservations about online courses were as follows: a fear of not being able to take the course, anger at not being able to understand the course, frustration at not being able to achieve their learning goal, disappointment with the instructors and administration, and general discomfort and unease whenever they had to do the course online.

7.10. Pedagogy and experience of online courses

It appears from our group interviews that many students did not have access to the online course platforms (Microsoft Teams) because of the difficulties they encountered in accessing an Internet connection on campus or at home. They also considered that the WhatsApp platform experimented with during the year was unsuitable for online courses.

Most students interviewed said they did not attend classes in ideal conditions because most of them lived with tutors. According to them, it was difficult to take courses at home because being at home and taking online courses was not something their tutors understood well.

The reasons given by the respondents for their difficulties in assimilating the courses were the following:

– inaccessibility and unavailability of course materials;

– the exchange time with the teacher for explanations lasted on average only 40 min;

– as a result, the explanations provided by the teachers were not satisfactory.

7.11. DSIC student critiques of the online training experience

The main criticisms DSIC students had of the online learning experience at UFHB were primarily related to the lack of real training in the effective use of WhatsApp and Microsoft Teams platforms in online courses.

In addition, not all students had access to these platforms. There was a lack of a free Internet connection on campus to facilitate access to online courses.

The length of the courses (30–45 min of class time, partly due to Internet connection problems) seemed to them to be insufficient for the amount of teaching time to which students were entitled.

Teachers seemed less accessible and available to them in the context of online courses. Students felt that teachers had become demotivated since the implementation of online courses. They also felt that the administration was not rigorous in organizing courses and assigning access codes to online course platforms.

7.12. Student suggestions for improving the organization of online courses

During our interviews, the students made suggestions to make virtual learning at UFHB sustainable. The main suggestions were as follows:

– include students in decisions that affect them;

– conduct a feasibility and market study to consider a range of factors that could affect the success of such an initiative;

– provide prior training for both teachers and students to ensure better ownership of online courses;

– subsidize Internet access for students to facilitate the ability to attend classes from home or any other location;

– ensure broad Internet coverage on campus.

It should be noted that a few weeks after the end of our survey, a boycott of online courses was initiated by the section of the Student and School Federation of Côte d'Ivoire (SSFCI) of the Information Communication and Arts Training and Research Unit (ICATRU) to which the DSIC belongs, to demand the end of the online training experience because it was conducted without sufficient investment. Among the most cited grievances were the volume of online courses, the difficulties in accessing the Internet on campus, and the difficulties encountered by some students in obtaining a valid institutional e-mail address to connect to the Teams platform to follow the online courses.

7.13. Discussion of the survey results

It appears from this exploratory study that one of the initial hypotheses made by some of the initiators of this online training experiment – that students were, for the most part, great users of digital technologies which would facilitate their adoption of online training – was not verified. Indeed, even before the idea of generalizing online training due to the Covid-19 pandemic was raised, some online learning practices were observed, such as the spontaneous creation of WhatsApp groups in each class by the students to facilitate, among other things, the sharing of documentation related to the different courses given to them. Yet, most students rejected this experience, mainly because of insufficient training and preparation. This rejection confirms that access to technology is insufficient to guarantee effective use. Indeed, as researchers such as DiMaggio and Hargittai (2002) have pointed out for some years now, the digital divide is no longer solely related to access to digital technologies but, above all, to the quality of the uses made of them. Nowadays, as Brotcorne and Valenduc (2009) point out, the issue of users' digital skills is becoming central. Our results show that DSIC students lamented a lack of training in the effective use of the online training platforms made available to them. It seemed obvious to some decision makers that because of the student's daily use of ICTs, generally for recreational purposes, it would be easy for them to adopt the online training project.

Moreover, their desire for training also concerned their teachers, who did not seem to have a sufficient command of these tools. On the other hand, the results of this study also expose the limits of the technological determinism that characterizes the discourse of certain decision makers in higher education in Côte d'Ivoire. Zacharia Tiemtoré (2007) criticizes an approach and describes it as a "utopia based on a mythical interpretation of technologies".

7.14. Conclusion

At the end of this study, we can note that in the era of the Covid-19 pandemic, virtual learning was identified as the ideal solution for the continuation of the training of UFHB students with respect to the restrictive measures that had been implemented, with major constraints and pitfalls that have not favored the success of this experience at DSIC.

Although this pandemic and its consequences on social life appeared to be an opportunity to finally succeed in the integration of digital technologies in university education at the FHB, it must be recognized that unpreparedness, lack of training and the cost and coverage of the Internet are all factors that have made the implementation of virtual learning at DSIC difficult and laborious. Although a favorable factor, the penetration of cell phones (smartphones) in the Ivorian university environment, especially among students, has not allowed optimal online courses.

However, it should be noted that although the DSIC abandoned this project after the student boycott of online courses, other departments of the UFHB (economics, modern literature), which experienced the same student movements, are still using the Teams' platform. In a future study, the conditions of the relative success of this experience in these departments should be investigated.

7.15. References

Bahi, A. (2006). Les universitaires ivoiriens et Internet. *Afrique et développement*, XLV, 3, 152–173.

Bahi, A. (2009). Étude sur les TIC et les pratiques de recherche d'information chez les enseignants et chercheurs universitaires ivoiriens, 2004 [Online]. Available at: http://www.codesria.org/Links/conferences/el_publ/elpubl_papers.htm [Accessed August 2009].

Bahi, A. and Gadou, D. (2008). Internet et enjeux de pouvoir dans le champ universitaire ivoirien [Online]. Available at: http://communication.revues.org/811 [Accessed 29 January 2014].

Bogui, M.J.-J. (2008). *Intégration et usages des technologies de l'information et de la communication dans l'éducation en Afrique : situation de l'enseignement supérieur en Côte d'Ivoire, 2003–2005.* Editions Édilivre, Paris.

Brotcorne, P. and Valenduc, G. (2009). Les compétences numériques et les inégalités dans les usages d'Internet. *Les cahiers du numérique*, 5(1), 45–68.

Ehile Ehouan, E. (2009). Le RÉÉSAO et la mise en œuvre du système LMD dans l'Espace UEMOA. Speech given on 22 April 2009 at Université Cheich Anta Diop, Dakar [Online]. Available at: http://www.ucad.sn/reesao/doc/reesao2013/communication/reesao_lmd.pdf [Accessed 2 April 2015].

Ekhauguere, G.O.S. (2000). L'enseignement supérieur en Afrique : défis et opportunités. Enseignement supérieur en Europe, XXV(3) [Online]. Available at: http://www.cepes.ro/publications/hee_french/3_2000/sommaire3.htm [Accessed May 2005].

Eszter, H. (2002). Second-level digital divide: Differences in people's online skills. *First Monday*, 7(4).

Glen, F. and Isaacs, S. (2007). Survey of ICT and education in Africa: A summary report, based on 53 country surveys [Online]. Available at: http://www.infoDev.org/en/Publication.353.html [Accessed June 15 2015].

Harvey, D. (1999). Les nouvelles technologies de l'information et des communications (TIC) et la formation universitaire. *Éducation et francophonie*, volume XXVII, No. 2, Autumn-Winter.

Karsenti, T. (2006). Comment favoriser la réussite des étudiants d'Afrique dans les formations ouvertes et à distance (foad) : principes pédagogiques. *TICE et développement* [Online]. Available at: http://www.revue-tice.info/doc [Accessed May 2006].

Karsenti, T. and Ngamo, S.T. (2007). Qualité de l'éducation en Afrique : le rôle potentiel des TIC. *International Review of Education*, 53(5), 665–686.

Leborgne-Tahiri, C. (2002). Universités et Nouvelles Technologies en Afrique de l'ouest francophone : passé, présent, et avenir. Bureau régionale de l'UNESCO à Dakar (BREDA).

Mian Bi, S.A. (2010). Usages et compétence TIC en formation initiale à l'ENS d'Abidjan (Côte d'Ivoire) : cas des formateurs et des futurs enseignants. PHD Thesis, Université de Montréal.

Moura A. and Carvalho, A.A. (2008). Génération mobile : environnement d'apprentissage supporté par des technologies mobiles (EASTM). *ilearning Forum 2008*, Paris.

Paul, D. and Eszter, H. (2002). From the "Digital Divide" to "Digital Inequality": Studying Internet use as penetration increases. Working paper, Princeton University Center for Arts and Cultural Policy Studies.

Rallet, A. and Rochelandet, F. (2004). La fracture numérique : une faille sans fondement ? *Réseaux*, 127–128, 19–54.

Raoul, B. (2001). L'internet, outil de développement : une nouvelle donnée pour l'éducation en Afrique noire. *Media Développement*, 48(1).

Roland, D. (2002). Université virtuelle, campus numérique… cautères sur jambe de bois ou facteurs déterminants de la refondation de l'enseignement supérieur en Afrique ? *Quelle université pour l'Afrique ?* MSHA, Pessac.

Tiemtore, Z. (2007). Les TIC dans l'éducation en Afrique sub-saharienne. Espoir fondé de développement ou émergence d'une nouvelle utopie ? [Online]. Available at: http://www.marsouin.org/IMG/pdf/Tiemtore_7-2007.pdf [Accessed 10 January 2016].

Traore, D. (2005). Quel avenir pour l'usage pédagogique des TIC en Afrique subsaharienne ? Cas de cinq pays membres du ROCARE. In *ICT and Changing Mindsets in Education*, Toure, K., Tchombe, T., Karsenti, T. (eds). Langaa, Bamenda.

UEMOA (2005). Étude sur l'enseignement supérieur dans les pays de l'UEMOA [Online]. Available at: http://www.uemoa.int/sites/default/files/bibliotheque/rapportenssuppii.pdf.

UNESCO (2013). Bulletin mensuel électronique du projet PADTICE. Bulletin, UNESCO.

8

The Use of ICT by Students of the University Ibn Zohr During Covid-19: Uses and Representations

To ensure pedagogical continuity in Morocco, measures were adapted in order to reach the objectives set before the pandemic. Modifications were made to different forms of learning, starting from face-to-face to online learning. Moroccan universities produced and adapted adequate materials to serve the students according to their favored learning styles. Online platforms were set up, MOOC courses were designed, video modules were recorded and even PPT presentations and PDF documents were disseminated. As for the students, on the other hand, they were trained and highly encouraged to acquire and deal with the "digital culture", considering their status as digital citizens.

8.1. Introduction

Digital technologies have changed our society by penetrating several spheres of social life to such an extent that more and more of our private time is being meshed with professional. The boundary between the private and the professional is becoming increasingly thin. Thus, the era of technological transition has affected and embraced practically all human activities (trade, education, administration, finance, security, leisure, sports, well-being and health). In this sense, Jauréguiberry and Proulx (2011) note that:

Chapter written by Abderrahmane AMSIDDER, Samar CHAKHRATI and Semaya EL BOUTOULY.

it is no longer possible today to think about the contemporary world without referring both to communication technologies that permeate it and to the upheavals in individual and collective behaviors related to the use of these technologies.

8.2. Contextualization

The Covid-19 pandemic caused a state of emergency worldwide, and Morocco, like other affected countries, declared the suspension of most activities in all sectors. During this period of crisis, and to ensure pedagogical continuity, all Moroccan universities opted for teaching adapted to the situation: from face-to-face to virtual learning or sometimes a combination of the two. In this chapter, we compare the results of two quantitative studies conducted at the University Ibn Zohr, Agadir, whose aim is to question the status of information and communication technologies (ICTs), particularly their use in a crisis in the Moroccan educational sector.

8.3. Objective

The primary objective of this chapter is to study the forms of ICT used among students in two academic institutions, through the prism of the Covid-19 pandemic. The first is open access: the Faculty of Letters and Human Sciences (FLHS); and the second is regulated access: the Higher School of Education and Training of Agadir (ESEFA).

8.4. Issue

Like other countries in the world, the Moroccan higher education sector has been affected by the Covid-19 pandemic. This situation led university officials to transition from traditional classroom-based teaching to virtual teaching, provided remotely via digital platforms. The objective was to ensure pedagogical continuity while avoiding blocking the sector at all costs (a wasted year with vast consequences).

In this contribution, we propose, through a comparison between an open-access institution and another with regulated access but belonging to the same university (University Ibn Zohr (UIZ) in Agadir, Morocco), to analyze the use of ICT by students from both institutions.

Our problem space revolves around two main questions:

– Q1: What use cases are likely to emerge from the participation of students in a virtual space that contains teaching devices made available to them by the university: video modules, pdf, PPT presentations, interactive activities?

– Q2: Do these devices contribute to the development of digital literacy among these same students?

Our reflection has three axes: the first axis is devoted to the definition of the concepts mobilized in our study, and the second axis exposes the methodological tools, and the main results of the two surveys carried out among the students at UIZ. Finally, the third axis is an opportunity to compare the forms of digital use among students at the two institutions.

8.5. Theoretical framework

As for the part devoted to the theoretical anchoring of our chapter, it seems judicious to reflect on the notion of "usage", given its interest in our chapter and the various meanings to which it gives rise.

The introduction of the concept of "usage" is part of a multidisciplinary framework since it comes from several disciplines, such as education sciences, cognitive psychology, information and communication sciences, sociology of usage and, more precisely, the theory of appropriation. The notion of usage has emerged in particular in the work of functionalist obedience (uses and gratifications) in the 1960s and 1970s. However, its use in other disciplinary fields has been accompanied by ongoing readjustment, leading researchers such as Paganelli (2012) to envision it as "a continuum of definitions from adoption to appropriation to use".

Thus, within the framework (Chambat, 1994) of this study, we consider the notion of use, following the example of Jouët as a social practice subject to determinants such as resistance to change, social habits, tradition, culture and the group of belonging.

Considering usage as a social practice allows us to break down the technical determinism that relegates the user to the background and overestimates the tool.

After these terminological clarifications, our purpose is to analyze the use of ICT by students of two institutions affiliated with the University Ibn Zohr: the ESEF and the FLSH.

8.6. Methodology and presentation of the tool

8.6.1. *Sample*

The data collected is based on two quantitative surveys: the first survey was conducted with 100 students at ESEF. In contrast, the second survey was conducted with 112 students enrolled in the French Studies program at FLSH.

8.6.2. *Questionnaire*

When developing the questionnaire, we took a few variables into consideration that we consider relevant to our analysis: notably gender, the type of program to which the students interviewed belong, and their place of residence. These variables allow us to verify the hypotheses put forward.

The questionnaire consists of five modules, with a total of 38 questions. We opted for closed questions, satisfaction questions and multiple-choice questions.

For data processing and analysis, we used descriptive and explanatory statistical techniques. The analysis of the questionnaire and the interpretation of the data were conducted through Google Forms and SPSS software, whose function is to process and analyze statistical data.

The survey includes noting the degree of students' digital exposure (degree of Internet connection) and the use of digital platforms related to teaching.

This pathway allowed us to highlight two distinct aspects regarding the place ICT and digital culture have in university students' lives during the lockdown period. In the first instance, we looked at digital platforms as a vector of media information and knowledge. The second aspect relates to the place that new technologies occupy within the student community.

Finally, it should be noted that the questionnaire was first tested on five students, but the results of this test are not included in this study.

8.7. Results and discussion

In what follows, we present the results of the two surveys descriptively and then discuss them based on comparing the two audiences.

– Distribution by gender:

Regarding male/female representation, the data collected from the first sample, that is, FLSH students, show that women represent more than 47%. The second sample (ESEF) data show a female presence of 48%.

– Place of residence:

The "environment" variable regarding the residence of the respondents is presented in Table 8.1.

	Rural area (%)	Urban environment (%)
FLSH students	45	55
ESEF students	41.50	58.50

Table 8.1. *Distribution of the respondents according to their place of residence*

Thus, most respondents are from urban areas, 55% for FLSH students, and over 58% for ESEF students.

8.7.1. *Some results related to the use and representations of ICT among students*

8.7.1.1. *Use and appropriation of ICT*

8.7.1.1.1. Possession of a mailbox

The possession of an email address reveals a significant degree of use of ICT in the student environment within the two institutions (96% at FLSH compared to 99% at ESEF). These results converge with those of a study conducted by Amsidder et al. (2014) on the practice, and use of ICT at Ibn Zohr University showed that most students have at least one email address. In our case, the trend shows that students in both institutions have several accounts on social networking sites, with WhatsApp, Facebook and Instagram dominating. It is also worth noting that Facebook is supplanted by WhatsApp for both audiences surveyed, with a slight difference for students (boys) from ESEF, where all three social networks are used equally. This dominance of WhatsApp in Morocco was confirmed by the annual report of the National Agency for Telecommunications Regulation[1], which revealed that 96.5% of Moroccans have a preference for WhatsApp.

8.7.1.1.2. Most used social networks versus gender

We also examined whether students use social networks, and found out which network is most favored by gender.

	WhatsApp	Facebook	Instagram	Twitter	YouTube	Other	Total
F	30	23	11	6	0	2	72
M	14	13	7	1	2	3	40
Total	44	36	18	7	2	5	112

Table 8.2. *Most used social networks versus gender – FLSH*

---

[1] ANRT, survey of ICT indicators collected from households and individuals at the national level for 2018, results from July 2019.

	WhatsApp	Facebook	Instagram	Twitter	YouTube	Other	Total
F	32	14	12	4	9	2	73
M	5	5	5	1	4	1	21
Total	37	19	17	5	13	3	94

Table 8.3. *Most used social networks versus gender – ESEF*

8.7.1.1.3. Access to ICT

The "In-person" mode seems most desired by most students.

	Remote (%)	MOOC (%)	Face-to-face (%)
FLSH students	35.40	30.40	55
ESEF students	31	15	54

Table 8.4. *Preferred mode of learning for students*

The results reveal that students from both institutions prefer the "face-to-face" mode, with a percentage equal to 55% at FLSH and 54% at ESEF. However, although they are "digital natives", few opt for "MOOCs". Their digital culture is, therefore, dissimilar to the uses prescribed by their institutions.

8.7.1.2. *Students' representations of ICT*

	Very satisfied (%)	Satisfied (%)	Moderately satisfied (%)	Not satisfied (%)	Not at all satisfied (%)
Students at FLSH	23.20	24.10	29.50	11.60	11.60
Students at ESEF	9.6	17	41.50	13.80	18.10

Table 8.5. *Satisfaction level of the measures taken by the establishment*

FLSH students point to their satisfaction with the measures taken by their institution, with a percentage of 23.20%, while we record that only 9.6% of their counterparts at ESEF are satisfied. Most respondents consider the measures taken by both institutions to be somewhat acceptable since they allow students to take their courses virtually.

8.7.1.3. *ICT and lockdown*

Access to the Internet has become available to all since 80.76% of FLSH students, compared to 70.58% of ESEF students, have access. The percentage of positive responses to this question is the highest. The high rates of Internet access highlight another issue, disparities between regions regarding the use of information and communication technologies, which we plan to address in a future study.

	Yes (%)	No (%)
FLSH students	42	58
ESEF students	48.90	51.10

Table 8.6. *Platform frequentation before lockdown*

The rate of use of the platforms by students before the lockdown is noteworthy. However, it also raises questions about whether the difficulties faced by students in the two populations when accessing the Internet are considered.

More than half of the FLSH respondents, according to Table 8.6, with a percentage of 58%, did not use the platforms compared to 51.10% of the ESEF respondents. However, a significant percentage of both samples does so, even before the lockdown.

The respondents were also asked to express the degree to which they used the platforms during the lockdown. The results confirm that students used the platforms to follow their courses virtually during this period, with a high rate reaching 85% among the students of the FLSH against 74% among those of the ESEF.

In terms of satisfaction, we note that a large majority of participants from both populations were moderately satisfied with the content posted on the platform, with a percentage that exceeds, in general, 35%. However, other students interviewed expressed great satisfaction with this content, with a percentage above 13%.

	Totally agree (%)	Agree (%)	Moderately agree (%)	Not in agreement (%)	Not at all in agreement (%)
FLSH students	44.60	17.90	19.60	12.50	5.40
ESEF students	6.40	11.70	23.40	22.30	36.20

Table 8.7. *The cost of accessing the Internet*

As we can see in Table 8.7, the majority of opinions converge. Indeed, about half of the respondents from the FLSH, at a percentage of 44.6%, find that accessing the Internet remains expensive. However, the population of ESEF thinks the opposite, with a significant percentage of 36.20%.

8.7.1.4. *Students' representations of ICT*

Social representation is a notion that occupies a central position in social psychology and human and social sciences. Since Serge Moscovici introduced it in 1961, it has been used increasingly. It is about the processes of constructing collective meanings that lead to common cognitions which produce links with society, organizations, and groups. However, Isambert and Moscovici (1961) define the notion as follows: "In a word, social representation is a particular modality of knowledge which has its function the elaboration of behaviors and communication between individuals".

Respondents from both samples have developed social representations regarding their use of ICT. The results of our study show that respondents from urban areas access the Internet through several means: smartphones are used by 46.77% of FLSH students compared to 56.36% of ESEF respondents. Meanwhile, rural residents use their smartphones to access the Internet, with a significant percentage reaching 60% of the population of the FLSH and 70% of the sample of those at ESEF who prefer to use them. The result is confirmed by the annual report of the ARNT[2] (2017): "Most Internet users prefer mobile connections, especially in rural areas".

It should be noted that the vast majority of participants in this survey confirmed that using ICT is complicated since this use requires infrastructure

---

2 National Agency of Telecommunication Regulation.

and equipment that remain expensive concerning the socioeconomic situation of the Moroccan student.

8.7.2. *Interpreting the survey results*

The objective of this chapter was to assess the impact of information and communication technologies on students at Ibn Zohr University, comparing their effect on FLSH students and ESEF students through the prism of the Covid-19 pandemic.

From the results above, we see that most participants have email and social network accounts, particularly Facebook and WhatsApp.

We also note that they are open to the Internet and ICT, possibly in teaching. Moreover, most are already surfing the Internet, regardless of the equipment used to access it, and they access the Internet regularly and continuously.

However, field investigations revealed a considerable digital divide between the place of residence of the participants and the equipment used to access the Internet. Ben Youssef (2004) further explains that:

> In the "broad sense", the digital divide is defined by the increase in the gap in ICT equipment (and access) between two given geographical areas or two given categories of individuals. It refers to a dividing line between territories (social groups) that have access to ICTs and those that do not have access or have it only marginally.

Furthermore, in addition to the lack of a good Internet connection in rural areas, the results also show that students in these areas do not have the necessary equipment to pursue online studies, since most of them, with a percentage of 62%, access learning through a smartphone.

8.8. Conclusion

Virtual learning represents a "revolution" for some and a "trend" for others. The answers of the questionnaire reveal a clear vision of virtual learning and the representations conceived by students about this so-called new form of education.

For Jouet (1997, p. 307):

> Representations are indeed forged in the confrontation with the technique, in the concrete use of the tools of communication. The statements of the individuals on the mode of concrete use of the devices translate their setting about the object. They pass by a language, often enameled with terms specific to the tools used and their terms, which reveal the ways of negotiating with the tool. They testify to forms of appropriating the object.

Learning, in this digital age, requires specific training to integrate information and communication technologies into teaching. This transition through training implies appropriating digital technology and redefining the new and expanded field of interaction that digital technology can offer. The consideration of training necessary for the appropriation of ICT creates a connection between the actors at the university level.

In conclusion, our exploratory study, quantitative by nature, allowed us to uncover the difference between the forms of use of ICT by students from an open-access institution: the FLSH; and their counterparts from a limited-access institution: the ESEF.

The results of our comparative study revealed the inexistence of clear differences between the use cases of the ICT in the two subject populations, given the quasi-similarity of the sociocultural conditions.

In general, most universities in Morocco have made platforms available to students which are considered spaces for study, exchange, the sharing of documents and communication. In addition to these measures, we also find many professors who have created their own spaces to post their courses on these platforms.

Moreover, this study opens up other perspectives. The present results can become the subject of other studies with another sample to evaluate the relevance of virtual learning, considering other variables exposed on a representative temporal interval.

8.9. References

Amsidder, A., Daghmi, F., Toumi, F. (2012). Usages et pratiques des publiques dans les pays du Sud. Des médias classiques au TIC. Université Ibn Zohr, Agadir.

Amsidder, A., Toumi, F., Youssoufi, K. (2014). Pratique et usage des TIC dans l'université Marocaine : le cas de l'université Ibn Zohr d'Agadir. *SFSIC* [Online]. Available at: https://sfsic2014.sciencesconf.org/ [Accessed 8 January 2023].

Basque, J. and Lundgren-Cayrol, K. (2002). Une typologie des typologies des applications des TIC en éducation. *Sciences et techniques éducatives*, 9(3), 263–289.

Ben Youssef, A. (2004). Les quatre dimensions de la fracture numérique. *Réseaux*, 127–128, 181–209.

Chambat, P. (1994). Usages des technologies de l'information et de la communication (TIC) : évolution des problématiques. *TIC et Sociétés*, 6(3), 249–270.

Collin, S., Guichon, N., Ntebutse, J.G. (2015). Une approche sociocritique des usages numériques en éducation. *Sciences et technologies de l'information et de la communication pour l'éducation et la formation*, 22(1), 89–117.

Cordier, A. (1999). Le livre numérique, Internet et la pensée. *Communication et langages*, 122(1), 11–18.

Daghmi, F., Pulvar, O., Toumi, F. (2012). Médias et publics au Maroc. *Les enjeux de l'information et de la communication*, 13/1(1), 86.

Drot-Delange, B. and Bruillard, R. (2012). Éducation aux TIC, cultures informatiques et du numérique : quelques repères historiques. *Études de communication*, 38, 69–80.

Isambert, F.A. and Moscovici, S. (1961). La psychanalyse, son image, son public. *Revue française de sociologie*, 2(4), 328.

Jouët, J. (1997). Pratiques de communication et figures de la médiation. Des médias de masse aux technologies de l'information et de la communication. *Sociologie de la communication*, 1(1), 291–312.

Jouët, J. (2000). Retour critique sur la sociologie des usages. *Réseaux*, 18(100), 487–521.

Lalli, P. (2005). Représentations sociales et communication. *Hermès La revue*, 41(1), 59.

Millerand, F. (1999). Usages des NTIC : les approches de la diffusion, de l'innovation et de l'appropriation. Université de Montréal.

Paganelli, C. (2012). Analyse des discours sur la notion d'"usage" dans deux revues en sciences de l'information : Doc-SI et BBF. *Documentaliste-Sciences de l'Information*, 49(2), 64.

Pronovost, G. (1994). Médias, éléments pour l'étude de la formation des usages sociaux. *Technologie de l'information et société*, 6(4), 377–400.

Proulx, S. (2002). Trajectoires d'usages des technologies de communication : les formes d'appropriation d'une culture numérique comme enjeu d'une "société du savoir". *Annales des télécommunications*, 57(3–4), 180–189.

Proulx, S. (2005). Penser les usages des TIC aujourd'hui : enjeux, modèles, tendances. *Presses universitaires de Bordeaux*, 1, 7–20.

Ripon, R. (2011). La mise en œuvre d'une enquête quantitative par questionnaire : vices et vertus du chiffre. *Presses de l'Enssib*, 1(22), 62–79.

Ségur, C. (2003). Philippe Breton, Serge Proulx, l'explosion de la communication à l'aube du XXIe siècle. *Questions de communication*, 4, 432–434.

9

Digital Communication for the Continuity of Socioeconomic Activities in Times of Covid-19 in Côte d'Ivoire: An Inventory of the Uses of ICTs

Covid-19 has impacted the way of life and functioning of individuals, administrations, companies and all social strata in Côte d'Ivoire. Indeed, following the measures put in place by authorities that implemented, among other measures, social distancing, these different entities have favored the use of digital tools in the framework of their organizational policies and the execution of their socio-professional or cultural activities. This qualitative study based on the theory of digital culture has shown that the use of digital tools has been thwarted by the preponderance of fake news surrounding the pandemic, the lack of mastery of these tools by the populations and the difficulties inherent in gaining access to digital tools. The study recommends the following actions to facilitate the accessibility of ICT for populations. It also recommends amplifying and extending education surrounding using ICTs at all levels of the school curriculum.

9.1. Introduction

As of November 23, 2021, in Côte d'Ivoire, communication No. 649 from the Ministry of Public Health, Hygiene and Universal Health Coverage revealed 61,652 confirmed cases and 703 deaths due to Covid-19.

Chapter written by Bassémory KONÉ.

Covid-19 thus appears as a dangerous and very contagious disease, and it left no choice but to maintain physical proximity. Therefore, to minimize the risk of spreading this disease, the authorities had to reinvent strategies while facilitating the continuity of socioeconomic activities. In addition, the evolution of Covid-19 led to a dysfunction of all socio-professional activities, including health services. Indeed, health services were perceived by the population as the main sources of Covid-19 contamination, and this poor perception led to a pronounced reluctance to use conventional health services. Most of the population gradually began to resort to self-medication as a preventive and curative measure, especially for malaria and the common cold. This approach became a primary resilience strategy, despite the serious health risks associated with this unrecommended practice (USAID 2020).

With regard to commercial activities, 94% of the heads of Informal Production Units (IPUs) believe that Covid-19 negatively affects their activities. Indeed, the production of industrial IPUs is down by 85%, their profits by 84% and customer orders by 81%. In addition, IPU's sales in March 2020 were down 82% from the same level in March 2019. This decrease in activity was reflected in a 62.5% decrease in the remuneration paid by IPUs and a 28% decrease in the cost of raw materials. Regarding the workforce, a total of 420,275 IPUs were affected by layoffs/unemployment of employees for 1,296,734 jobs lost, reaching a total estimated job loss of 39% (Ahouré et al. 2021, p. 34).

Social distancing was necessary to ensure the continuity of activities. Communication channels were used to manage the health crisis and disseminate information on the disease and preventative measures. But managing this health crisis also requires reorganizing the modes of organizing work, considering the interpersonal relations inherent in socioeconomic activities. This reinvention of managerial approaches needs to be understood and analyzed to enrich knowledge and improve the capacity of organizations to anticipate crisis management. Indeed, the socioeconomic situation caused by the health crisis *constitutes a constantly evolving target.*

This study focuses on digital communication in managerial practices. It is important to understand and analyze the contribution of digital communication when it comes to how new managerial approaches were adapted so that socioeconomic activities could continue. How did digital communication contribute to adapting innovative managerial approaches so socioeconomic activities could continue during Covid-19 in Côte d'Ivoire?

First, answering the above question leads us to present the deployment of digital communication in socioeconomic mutations generated by the unexpected advent of Covid-19. Second, it allows us to identify key obstacles and highlight recommendations to better adapt to managerial approaches.

We postulate that the effectiveness of innovative managerial practices consistently depends on implementing a device in education to enable dynamic digital transformation. This device allows us to understand the obstacles and highlight ideas and strategies to overcome them to boost the resilience of activities within a socioeconomic dynamic. ADEA (2021) emphasizes the imperative to rethink how to ensure, for example, quality education equitably and inclusively. Technology represents one of the key enablers.

9.2. Key theories

Digital culture refers to the knowledge about all new configurations of public space, forms of internet democracy and the influence of algorithms and search engines (Cardon 2019). It is a question of developing a collective reflection on the impact of digital devices on the renewal of informational and communicational practices for users. For Cardon, this renewal of info-communication practices due to digital devices results from the computerization of society (Vayre 2019). Cardon traces the history of the development of the Internet and the Web, showing how the success that technologies have experienced depends on how they have combined with society. Cardon invites economic and social actors to acquire skills and tools to better understand how the digital world shapes society. The theory of digital culture traces a path to reflect on economic and political actors, teachers and researchers, and citizens regarding how society can influence digital practices. Three aspects are proposed in this regard: the increase in the power of individuals through digital technology, the appearance of new and original collective forms and the redistribution of power and value. We should not neglect the fact that the Internet comprises a set of technologies that, since their origins, can favor both the alienation and emancipation of individuals.

We perform a Swot analysis of digital communication in Côte d'Ivoire and its deployment in the Covid-19 response plan to put a system in place that considers both the weaknesses and strengths.

9.3. Method

This study is based on a literature review and a qualitative study. It consisted of collecting and analyzing scientific articles, official releases, press articles and publications on digital social networks related to the management of Covid-19 until the end of November 2021. It also describes the deployment and effects of digital communication among populations. To this end, it was necessary to interview people in public places: markets, public transportation, train stations and secondary and university institutions. Also, publications on the management of Covid-19 should be surveyed.

9.4. The deployment of digital communication for socioeconomic activities

The health shock triggered by Covid-19 has led the state of Côte d'Ivoire, like other countries in the world, to reinvent itself to deal with the pandemic. Above all, digital technology represents the ideal channel to continue socioeconomic activities, even political-administrative and cultural activities. In this case, deploying digital communication cannot be optional; it relies on making progress. There has been an acceleration of digital transformation, which refers to the diffusion and use of digital technologies (the Internet, cell phones and other tools and systems) to digitally collect, store, analyze and exchange information (World Bank 2016; Brookings 2017).

This deployment was observed at the level of political-administrative activities, the level of the education/training sector, the level of businesses, the level of religious activities and then at the level of traditional-modern activities.

9.4.1. *Political-administrative activities in times of Covid-19*

The political and administrative authorities wasted no time in interrupting face-to-face activities. All public gathering places were closed less than a week after the first case was confirmed. Gatherings, if they were to take place, were to be held in open areas, and the number of participants was not to exceed 50 people. Participants were to be separated by at least 1 m. To set an example, the government postponed holding face-to-face meetings within the council of government and ministers. Most or almost all of the meetings that were to take place were held online. The use of digital means has provided "additional tools to respond to the Covid-19 pandemic". Undoubtedly, digital platforms "facilitated the rapid development of social protection programs and enabled the maintenance of some essential public services" (Long and Ascent 2020).

At the level of general administration, many public organizations allowed most of their workers to work from home, except for the defense and security forces and health workers. Different platforms were used to share information. Public bodies marked their presence on digital social networks by increasingly publishing on existing platforms and new platforms created for this purpose. This was the case of the Ministry of Health and Public Hygiene, at the forefront of the resistance against Covid-19. The Ministry of Health, at the forefront of the fight, set up interactive information platforms providing information about Covid-19. In addition to these platforms, awareness-raising SMS messages were sent to the various subscribers of cell phone operators.

The IMF (Long and Ascent 2020) observed that some countries were making cash transfers using mobile money to provide immediate and much-needed support to those affected by the pandemic. In the case of Côte d'Ivoire, the government's financial support fund for the population was distributed by the Ministry of Solidarity and Social Cohesion, through mobile banking, to people affected by the pandemic. It was also through digital means that eligible households received credit for electrical energy for their card meter, as the President of the Republic promised.

At the level of public service, the new biometric passport agency made efforts to offer online services, including applications, appointment scheduling and payments.

The government recommended that business leaders follow suit. Thus, employees who did not need to be present at the workplace could telework. Companies, therefore, turned to digital means to maintain internal communication and external relations.

9.4.2. *Digital technology at the service of companies*

Digital transformation partially allowed Ivorian companies to maintain their activity during the Covid-19 pandemic. This chapter shows how companies use digital means. Companies in the manufacturing sector are increasingly turning to the use of artificial intelligence to boost their production. However, a significant part of the task requires human intervention. Where human labor is indispensable, there is no other option. However, workers were allowed to work from home in areas where tasks could be performed remotely. These workers had to be in touch with their respective management. To this end, the government recommends that cell phone operators facilitate telecommuting by providing a quality service. Among all areas, commercial services have been the most active in digital communication to maintain contact with customers and increase their portfolios.

9.4.2.1. *Online services*

Online service has increased in the service sector. From banks to insurance companies, customers are increasingly benefiting from remote services. Many digital services are available to them, and the health crisis has only accentuated these services. For example, using the services offered by banks and insurance has not proven too difficult, whether for customer advice, statements or balance requests, withdrawals or transfer requests.

9.4.2.2. *Online sales*

Doing business online helped companies to stay afloat. Despite offices closing or almost closing, it was necessary to continue supplying customers. Sales and deliveries were made via digital means. Even if big companies were increasingly present in the market, we saw a rise in online stores. This is due to the growing interest in entrepreneurship. Indeed, several young people had already launched product distribution services (beauty, food, household appliances). In addition are those who were obliged to launch an online business to survive. In addition, 11.8% of businesses in the accommodation and catering industry had to close their sales outlets. Workers for many businesses in industrial zones, hotels, restaurants and maquis had no income. This was because all activities had been abruptly interrupted in the companies that employed them (Ahouré et al. 2021).

9.4.3. *Online courses in the education/training sector*

The closure of educational institutions as part of the response to Covid-19 lasted from March 16 to May 24, 2020. No preschool, school, secondary, technical or higher education establishments were open during this period. Cities in the greater Abidjan area were isolated from other cities. It was necessary to resort to an alternative measure so that primary, secondary and university education could continue. Thus, government authorities initiated online courses in accordance with the digital policy instituted in 2015 (Djede and Adon 2021).

The initiatives "intersect to ensure the continuity of teaching, mobilizing either the national media, especially radio and television, or social networks and more generally ICT and digital" (Yapi-Diahou 2020, p. 102).

Learning sessions were recorded and broadcast for primary and secondary education on national radio and TV channels. These sessions were also accessible via the Internet through terminals on dedicated platforms. Learners had the opportunity to follow these courses, to do exercises and personal research to deepen their knowledge. Older students, that is, those in secondary school, could follow courses organized by their teachers or do exercises via WhatsApp groups. These courses on WhatsApp were organized individually by teachers for others at the school administration's request. These were very commendable initiatives (Koffi-Didia 2020) that contributed to strengthening the training of students in this particular context of lockdown, which the closure of schools has characterized.

As far as higher education is concerned, the health crisis was a springboard to accelerate the digital policy implemented in 2015. Indeed, the decree which created the Virtual University of Côte d'Ivoire (UVCI), Decree No. 2015-775 of December 9, 2015, theoretically enshrines the emergence of digital policy in Ivorian higher education. This digital policy was supposed to correct the dysfunctions of the Ivorian higher education sector. These dysfunctions are, "among others, the inadequacy and obsolescence of school and social infrastructures, the overcrowding of universities, the inadequacy and obsolescence of equipment and teaching and research materials" (Djede and Adon 2021). It is these dysfunctions that made the reputation of Ivorian higher education institutions decline over the years. It was therefore planned as part of its infrastructural rehabilitation to re-equip educational spaces with computer tools and ICT, and to implement digital projects, in this case regarding accessibility to scientific and technical information for teachers and students (PERI), and the project of the Ivorian Telecommunication Network for Education and Research (RITER) (Djede and Adon 2021). While it is true that Ivorian academics were using digital technology to access electronic networks, specialized online journals, computer libraries and databases of world universities, they lacked training in using ICT in their teaching practices (Djede and Adon 2021). This need for training and re-equipping with computer and ICT tools was not met until universities were closed due to Covid-19.

At UVCI, Covid-19 did not affect activities being carried out, given that this University is designed to provide online courses. According to its director, Tiémoman Koné,

> UVCI continues to operate normally. The measures taken by the state as part of the Covid-19 health emergency have not harmed the smooth running of our courses. This is because we are a university with a techno-pedagogical model of virtual learning that allows any learner to learn from anywhere and at any time (Ministry of Higher Education and Scientific Research 2020).

Concerning other public universities, teachers, at the request of university authorities, made digital materials of their courses and tutorials, practical work and lectures available to their students. These materials were to be emailed or published in student WhatsApp groups. They were also asked to record explanations on a digital medium in a small number of students' presence and make them available to the students. The students were, in turn, asked to send in comments and concerns about any areas of uncertainty. The teacher was then to collect this feedback and make another recording to provide clarification.

9.4.3.1. *Digital technology as a vector for the continuity of social dynamism*

Digital technology has been of great support to maintaining social dynamism. Below is the testimony of a teacher-researcher, and mother.

NICTs were already present in our lives before the lockdown, but they have become even more so. This is reflected in our daily use of cell phones for telephone communications with relatives, friends, and colleagues, digital messaging via the Internet, WhatsApp, and a high consumption of media (TV, movies, radio) that allows us to follow information about the pandemic at the local, national and international level.

In what follows, particular emphasis is placed on using ICTs for worship services and funeral management. Indeed, at these two levels of social dynamism, mobilization is strong. Moreover, the need to be in contact with other people is even stronger to survive.

9.4.4. Religious services

With places of worship closed, religious leaders and guides took advantage of the digital transformation to stay in touch with their followers. Thus, moments of prayer were broadcast live to allow the faithful to receive the support they needed. These broadcasts were accessible on smartphones, and WhatsApp groups or Facebook rooms were created for the occasion. This allowed many faithful people to keep their spiritual flame lit in their lives and homes.

9.4.4.1. ICT for funeral management

As Agnès Gnammon-Adiko explained, the moment of mourning, according to which death is "this commonplace and the funeral that it entails is a social and cultural fact in all societies, targeted by the Covid-19 measures". However, it is when we feel a moral duty to show relatives and acquaintances a level of support. But given the measures, it was necessary to stay physically distant and mourn individually. This is where the advantage of digital transformation came in. Instead of physical meetings to make decisions within the organization's framework, virtual meetings were held for the different stages of funeral preparation. In the context of mobilizing funds to support the funeral organization, mobile banking was used in the absence of physical visits to hand over someone's share of the contribution directly.

For the different rituals, terminals were broadcast live so everyone could follow the different stages: wakes, moving the body, requiem mass or funeral services and burials.

9.4.5. *Identified obstacles*

Digital transformation was certainly very useful in response to Covid-19 in Côte d'Ivoire. However, the country could have benefited greatly from digital transformation if the authorities had put digital communication at the heart of the response strategy. For example, applicants for exit permits from the greater Abidjan area were forced to crowd in front of the National Police School in Cocody. A platform should have been set up for this purpose. Neglecting the power of digital communication has created some noise among the population. Indeed, the digital transformation has also spearheaded the infodemic. It greatly facilitated the spread of fake news, drowning out reliable information about the disease. These rumors disrupted the management of the response.

Also, media literacy, specifically new media, was not considered when the training curriculum was a huge problem in the transition to online courses. Many teachers and students did not know how to use the devices for online courses.

For those who mastered the digital tools, there was the problem of having the equipment or a reliable connection. Below we have a testimony from a mother and teacher on the difficulties encountered by children during the period in which educational institutions were closed.

> Implementation requires permanent access to means and tools of Internet connection for all, students and teachers, but also parents [...] during a course by videoconference with her math teacher, my daughter exclaimed, "Hey, the course has stopped. They cut the current at Mr. T. B.". Then a few minutes later, the power was restored, and the class resumed. Another time, a student asked the teacher for a little more time at the end of a video conference assignment due immediately. The student used up her credit and needs the time to purchase connection

credits at the store next door. These real-life situations can be barriers to the continued spread of digital education.

9.5. Recommendations to better adapt digital communication to managerial approaches

It is important to better adapt digital communication to managerial approaches so that the mastery of digital tools is among the skills to be acquired during their career.

9.5.1. *A greater commitment from the state*

It is the responsibility of the state to provide educational institutions with the necessary equipment to acquire this skill. Also, the state must promote the acquisition of digital tools in households and guarantee electricity supplies. In addition, the state must review training programs for citizens to consider the skills that can help future managers to meet the challenges ahead.

It is important to dematerialize procedures related to Covid-19, such as appointments for vaccinations, tests, or test results, to avoid repeating the situation experienced by applicants for exit permits in the greater Abidjan area, who were forced to crowd in front of the National Police School in Cocody.

9.5.2. *Greater involvement of civil society*

Given the number of people who do not know how to use terminals or those who use them wrongly, it is up to consumer organizations and NGOs to direct their actions toward extensive and adequate use of digital technology. To do so, civil society leaders must carry out actions to advocate in favor of the digital culture. In concrete terms, this means advocating for the reduction of costs related to the use of the Internet and a subsidy so that people can acquire digital equipment.

In addition, civil society leaders must get involved and support the state to create an education mechanism so that ICT can be better used. This is necessary to build shields for populations that allow them to resist false information and, therefore, take better advantage of these communication tools and fight against social problems.

9.6. Conclusion

Deploying digital communication has helped weaken the shocks caused by the health crisis. Digital communication has contributed to the governance of the response to Covid-19, especially regarding disseminating information on the disease. It has also helped to maintain socioeconomic dynamism. Digital transformation has facilitated teleworking and allowed businesses to continue their activities for the benefit of the population. Even at the cultural level, digital communication has been used to organize rituals related to the life of traditional societies.

However, the fact that it has been used without testing has led to problems. It is now necessary to evaluate the obstacles and take them into account for more dynamic digital communication, which can be useful for the resilience of organizations during sociopolitical unrest or health pandemics.

9.7. References

ADEA (2020). Impact de la Covid-19 sur l'éducation en Afrique. Final report, ADEA, Abidjan.

Aga, S.S., Khan, M.A., Nissar, S.S., Banday, M.Z. (2020). Evaluation de la santé mentale et des diverses stratégies d'adaptation dans la population générale vivant sous l'emprise de la Covid-19 à travers le monde : une étude transversale. *Ethics, Medecine and Public Health*, 15.

Apedjinou, A. and Ayayi, K.C.A. (2020). Jeunesse et numérique en Afrique : rôle de l'école pour une attitude critique et réflexive dans l'usage des réseaux sociaux. *Assempe*, no. 16, December.

Cardon, D. (2019). *Culture numérique*. Presses de Sciences Po, Paris.

Coulibaly, M. (2019). Les obstacles à l'usage des TIC par les enseignants en Côte d'Ivoire : cas de l'enseignement secondaire. Thesis, Université de Haute Alsace, Mulhouse.

Diouf, I., Bousso, A., Sonko, I. (2020). Gestion de la pandémie Covid 19 au Sénégal. *Médecine de Catastrophe – Urgences Collectives*, 4(3), 217–222.

Djede, A.J. and Adon, K.P. (2021). La relance de la politique numérique dans l'enseignement supérieur ivoirien pendant la crise sanitaire de la Covid-19. *Revue internationale des technologies en pédagogie universitaire/International Journal of Technologies in Higher Education*, 18(1), 75–88.

Fogha, J.V.F. and Noubiap, J.J. (2020). La lutte contre le Covid-19 au Cameroun nécessite un second souffle. *Pan African Medical Journal*, 37(14).

Henry, B. (2018). Préparation du Canada en cas de grippe pandémique : stratégie de communication. *Relevé des maladies transmissibles au Canada*, 44(5), 118–122.

Hoummadi, L., Hafid, J., Machraoui, S., Admou, B. (2020). Jusqu'où l'Afrique peut-elle limiter les impacts de la Covid 19. *Revue d'épidémiologie et de santé publique*, 68, 302–305.

Karsenti, T. and Collin, S. (2012). Using IT for distance learning: Benefits and challenges for African learners. *Teachers & Teaching*, 20(2), 9–18.

Kassoum, T. and Memon, F. (2020). Causes et expressions de la propagation rapide du nouveau coronavirus "Covid-19" en Côte d'Ivoire. *European Journal of Social Sciences Studies*, 5(2).

Koffi-Didia, A.M. (2020). Mon cahier COVID 19 au quotidien : "Coronavirus quand tu nous tiens !". Témoignages et questionnements en Afrique subsaharienne. In Cahier "COVID 19 au quotidien", Yapi-Diahou, A. (ed.). hal-02859844.

Kone, M.G.R., Affi, S.T., Bede, A.L., Assoma, A.B., Konate, B., Ziao, N. (2020). Évolution prévisionnelle de la pandémie du Covid-19 en République de Côte d'Ivoire : analyse statistique factuelle. *Afrique Science*, 16(5), 1–7.

Long, A. and Ascent, D. (2020). World economic outlook. Report, International Monetary Fund, 177.

Mian Bi, S.A. (2019). Usages du groupe Facebook en situation de stage : le cas des éducateurs de l'ENS d'Abidjan. *Formation et profession*, 27(1), 70–83.

Monnier, A. (2020). Covid-19 : de la pandémie à l'infodémie et la chasse aux fake news. *Recherches & éducations* [Online]. Available at: https://doi.org/10.4000/rechercheseducations.9898.

Ndiaye, M. and Diatta, A.E.R. (2020). Procédure de dépistage d'une infection à Covid-19 en milieu de travail structuré africain. *Archives des Maladies Professionnelles et de l'Environnement*, 81, 337–340.

Oyeniran, O.I., Chia, T., Oraebosi, M.I. (2020). Combating Covid-19 pandemic in Africa: An urgent call to scale up laboratory testing capacities. *Ethics, Medicine, and Public Health*, 15, 100552.

Revue Économie, Gestion et Société (2020). La crise pandémique de Coronavirus. Acte des webinaires de l'Ecole Supérieure de Technologie de Meknès-Maroc.

Semporé, E., Bazié, H., Ilboudo, B., Kpoda, H., Bila, B., Somé, T., Sossa, O., Méda, C., Hien, H. (2020). Comment prendre le pas sur le coronavirus dans un pays en développement : questions et actions au Burkina Faso. *The Pan African Medical Journal*, 35(Supp. 2), 37.

UN-Habitat (2020). La Covid-19 dans les villes africaines : impacts, ripostes et recommandations politiques. Report, UN-Habitat.

USAID (2020). Analyse qualitative, maladie à coronavirus (Covid 19) en Côte d'Ivoire, quelles conséquences sur les ménages vulnérables et les services sociaux de base [Online]. Available at: https://www.unicef.org/evaluation/media/2201/file/Rapport%20recherche:%20Maladie%20%C3%A0%20Coronavirus%20en%20C%C3%B4te%20d'Ivoire.pdf [Accessed 12 January 2022].

Villasenor, J.D., West, D.M., Lewis, R.J. (2016). The 2016 Brookings financial and digital inclusion project report: Advancing equitable financial ecosystems. Report, Brookings, Washington, DC.

Vignaux, P. and Prieto, N. (2020). Impact psychique de la pandémie de Covid-19 sur les professionnels soignants. *Actualités Pharmaceutiques*, 599, 51–53.

WHO (2008). Guide de l'OMS sur la planification de la communication lors des flambées de maladies.

WHO (2018). Communication du risque pendant les urgences sanitaires : directives stratégiques et pratiques de l'OMS pour la communication sur les risques en situation d'urgence.

WHO (2020a). Lutte contre la propagation de la Covid-19 aux postes-frontières : orientations provisoires. 20 May.

WHO (2020b). Promouvoir les mesures de santé publique dans le cadre de la riposte à la Covid-19 sur les cargos et les navires de pêche : orientations provisoires. 25 August.

World Bank Group (2016). World development report 2016: Digital dividends. Report, World Bank Publications.

Yapi-Diahou, A. (2020). Cahier "COVID 19 au quotidien". hal-02859844.

Zahonogo, P. (2021). Impacts des politiques publiques liées a la pandémie de la Covid 19 sur le secteur informel, les femmes et les jeunes : cas du Burkina Faso, du Cameroun, de la Côte d'Ivoire et du Sénégal : desktop review du Burkina-Faso.

List of Authors

Abderrahmane AMSIDDER
Laboratoire de recherche sur les
langues et la communication
(LARLANCO)
Ibn Zohr University
Agadir
and
Centre National Pour la Recherche
Scientifique et Technique (CNRST)
Rabat
and
Agence Nationale d'Evaluation et
d'Assurance Qualité (ANEAQ)
Rabat
and
Moroccan Association of Information
and Communication Sciences
Morocco

Julien ATCHOUA
Université Félix Houphouët-Boigny
Abidjan
Côte d'Ivoire

Marcel BAGARE
Information and Communication
Sciences (ICS)
École Normale Supérieure de
Koudougou (ENSK)
Burkina Faso

Jean-Jacques Maomra BOGUI
UFR Information, Communication
and Arts
Université Félix Houphouët-Boigny
Abidjan
Côte d'Ivoire

Samar CHAKHRATI
University Ibn Zohr
Agadir
Morocco

Nanga Désiré COULIBALY
Université Félix Houphouët-Boigny
Abidjan
Côte d'Ivoire

Saikou DIALLO
Old Dominion University (ODU)
Virginia
USA

Semaya EL BOUTOULY
University Ibn Zohr
Agadir
Morocco

Losséni FANNY
University of Korhogo
Côte d'Ivoire

Bassémory KONÉ
UFR Information and
Communication Sciences
UFR Information, Communication
and Arts
Department of Communication
Center for Communication Studies
and Research (CERCOM)
Laboratory of Communication
Sciences, Arts and Culture
University Félix Houphouët-Boigny
Abidjan
Côte d'Ivoire

Hanane MABROUK
Laboratoire de recherche sur les
langues et la communication
(LARLANCO)
Ibn Zohr University
Agadir
Morocco

Mohamed SALIOU CAMARA
Department of African Studies
Howard University
Washington, DC
USA

Youssouf SOUMAHORO
Information and Communication
Sciences
Université Félix Houphouët-Boigny
Abidjan
Côte d'Ivoire

John VAN DEN PLAS
Lab-network ULYSSE
Ecsedi-Isalt
Brussels
Belgium

Index

A

activities
  business, 152
  cultural, 147, 150, 155, 158
  education/training, 153
  political-administrative, 150, 151
  religious, 150, 155
awareness, 61, 63, 67, 68, 71–73, 75

C, D

crisis, 61, 62, 64–71, 74, 75
digital
  communication, 148–150, 152, 156–158
  culture, 147, 149, 157
  technologies, 15–20, 22, 23, 29, 30, 117–121, 128, 129
    ambivalence about the uses, 15, 20, 27–29
distance learning, 133, 134, 142, 143

E, F, H

e-learning, 117
everyday, 5, 8
fake news, 33–53
health crisis, 35, 50, 53

I, M, O, P

ICT, 3–8, 10, 13
  use, 134–136, 138, 140, 141
Instagram, 95, 105, 109–111
media, 86
musical works, 62–65, 67, 70–72
ordinary courtyard, 3, 5, 13
pedagogical continuity, 133, 134
protection, 85, 90, 93
public communication, 19, 20, 22, 27, 28

R, S

reinvention, 79, 80, 86, 88, 93
rumors, 15, 17, 22–27, 29
second-degree digital divide, 121, 122, 128

social networks, 33, 35–38, 40–42, 44, 47, 49–53, 86, 88, 89, 93
surfing, 95–105, 108–112

T, U, V

theatre, 81–84, 88, 90–93
tourism, 95–98, 100–103, 105, 106, 108, 112
University Félix Houphouët-Boigny (UFHB), 117, 119, 123, 124, 126, 127, 129
users, 3, 4, 6, 7, 11–13
vaccine, 33, 35–38, 43–52

Other titles from

in

Systems and Industrial Engineering – Robotics

2023

CHAINEAUX Jacques
The Mechanisms of Explosions: 27 Case Studies for their Understanding

2022

AMARA Yacine, BEN AHMED Hamid, GABSI Mohamed
Hybrid Excited Synchronous Machines: Topologies, Design and Analysis

BOURRIÈRES Jean-Paul, PINÈDE Nathalie, TRAORÉ Mamadou Kaba, ZACHAREWICZ Grégory
From Logistic Networks to Social Networks: Similarities, Specificities, Modeling, Evaluation

DEMOLY Frédéric, ANDRÉ Jean-Claude
4D Printing 1: Between Disruptive Research and Industrial Applications
4D Printing 2: Between Science and Technology

HAJJI Rafika, JARAR OULIDI Hassane
Building Information Modeling for a Smart and Sustainable Urban Space

KROB Daniel
Model-based Systems Architecting: Using CESAM to Architect Complex Systems
(Systems of Systems Complexity Set – Volume 3)

LOUIS Gilles
Dynamics of Aircraft Flight

2020

BRON Jean-Yves
System Requirements Engineering

KRYSINSKI TOMASZ, MALBURET FRANÇOIS
Energy and Motorization in the Automotive and Aeronautics Industries

PRINTZ Jacques
System Architecture and Complexity: Contribution of Systems of Systems to Systems Thinking

2019

ANDRÉ Jean-Claude
Industry 4.0: Paradoxes and Conflicts

BENSALAH Mounir, ELOUADI Abdelmajid, MHARZI Hassan
Railway Information Modeling RIM: The Track to Rail Modernization

BLUA Philippe, YALAOU Farouk, AMODEO Lionel, DE BLOCK Michaël, LAPLANCHE David
Hospital Logistics and e-Management: Digital Transition and Revolution

BRIFFAUT Jean-Pierre
From Complexity in the Natural Sciences to Complexity in Operations Management Systems
(Systems of Systems Complexity Set – Volume 1)

BUDINGER Marc, HAZYUK Ion, COÏC Clément
Multi-Physics Modeling of Technological Systems

FLAUS Jean-Marie
Cybersecurity of Industrial Systems

JAULIN Luc
Mobile Robotics – Second Edition Revised and Updated

KUMAR Kaushik, DAVIM Paulo J.
Optimization for Engineering Problems

TRIGEASSOU Jean-Claude, MAAMRI Nezha
Analysis, Modeling and Stability of Fractional Order Differential Systems 1: The Infinite State Approach
Analysis, Modeling and Stability of Fractional Order Differential Systems 2: The Infinite State Approach

VANDERHAEGEN Frédéric, MAAOUI Choubeila, SALLAK Mohamed, BERDJAG Denis
Automation Challenges of Socio-technical Systems

2018

BERRAH Lamia, CLIVILLÉ Vincent, FOULLOY Laurent
Industrial Objectives and Industrial Performance: Concepts and Fuzzy Handling

GONZALEZ-FELIU Jesus
Sustainable Urban Logistics: Planning and Evaluation

GROUS Ammar
Applied Mechanical Design

LEROY Alain
Production Availability and Reliability: Use in the Oil and Gas Industry

MARÉ Jean-Charles
Aerospace Actuators 3: European Commercial Aircraft and Tiltrotor Aircraft

MAXA Jean-Aimé, BEN MAHMOUD Mohamed Slim, LARRIEU Nicolas
Model-driven Development for Embedded Software: Application to Communications for Drone Swarm

MBIHI Jean
Analog Automation and Digital Feedback Control Techniques
Advanced Techniques and Technology of Computer-Aided Feedback Control

MORANA Joëlle
Logistics

SIMON Christophe, WEBER Philippe, SALLAK Mohamed
Data Uncertainty and Important Measures
(Systems Dependability Assessment Set – Volume 3)

TANIGUCHI Eiichi, THOMPSON Russell G.
City Logistics 1: New Opportunities and Challenges
City Logistics 2: Modeling and Planning Initiatives
City Logistics 3: Towards Sustainable and Liveable Cities

ZELM Martin, JAEKEL Frank-Walter, DOUMEINGTS Guy, WOLLSCHLAEGER Martin
Enterprise Interoperability: Smart Services and Business Impact of Enterprise Interoperability

2017

ANDRÉ Jean-Claude
From Additive Manufacturing to 3D/4D Printing 1: From Concepts to Achievements
From Additive Manufacturing to 3D/4D Printing 2: Current Techniques, Improvements and their Limitations
From Additive Manufacturing to 3D/4D Printing 3: Breakthrough Innovations: Programmable Material, 4D Printing and Bio-printing

ARCHIMÈDE Bernard, VALLESPIR Bruno
Enterprise Interoperability: INTEROP-PGSO Vision

CAMMAN Christelle, FIORE Claude, LIVOLSI Laurent, QUERRO Pascal
Supply Chain Management and Business Performance: The VASC Model

FEYEL Philippe
Robust Control, Optimization with Metaheuristics

MARÉ Jean-Charles
Aerospace Actuators 2: Signal-by-Wire and Power-by-Wire

POPESCU Dumitru, AMIRA Gharbi, STEFANOIU Dan, BORNE Pierre
Process Control Design for Industrial Applications

RÉVEILLAC Jean-Michel
Modeling and Simulation of Logistics Flows 1: Theory and Fundamentals
Modeling and Simulation of Logistics Flows 2: Dashboards, Traffic Planning and Management
Modeling and Simulation of Logistics Flows 3: Discrete and Continuous Flows in 2D/3D

2016

ANDRÉ Michel, SAMARAS Zissis
Energy and Environment
(Research for Innovative Transports Set – Volume 1)

AUBRY Jean-François, BRINZEI Nicolae, MAZOUNI Mohammed-Habib
Systems Dependability Assessment: Benefits of Petri Net Models
(Systems Dependability Assessment Set – Volume 1)

BLANQUART Corinne, CLAUSEN Uwe, JACOB Bernard
Towards Innovative Freight and Logistics
(Research for Innovative Transports Set – Volume 2)

COHEN Simon, YANNIS George
Traffic Management
(Research for Innovative Transports Set – Volume 3)

MARÉ Jean-Charles
Aerospace Actuators 1: Needs, Reliability and Hydraulic Power Solutions

REZG Nidhal, HAJEJ Zied, BOSCHIAN-CAMPANER Valerio
Production and Maintenance Optimization Problems: Logistic Constraints and Leasing Warranty Services

TORRENTI Jean-Michel, LA TORRE Francesca
Materials and Infrastructures 1
(Research for Innovative Transports Set – Volume 5A)
Materials and Infrastructures 2
(Research for Innovative Transports Set – Volume 5B)

WEBER Philippe, SIMON Christophe
Benefits of Bayesian Network Models
(Systems Dependability Assessment Set – Volume 2)

YANNIS George, COHEN Simon
Traffic Safety
(Research for Innovative Transports Set – Volume 4)

2015

AUBRY Jean-François, BRINZEI Nicolae
Systems Dependability Assessment: Modeling with Graphs and Finite State Automata

BOULANGER Jean-Louis
CENELEC 50128 and IEC 62279 Standards

BRIFFAUT Jean-Pierre
E-Enabled Operations Management

MISSIKOFF Michele, CANDUCCI Massimo, MAIDEN Neil
Enterprise Innovation

2014

CHETTO Maryline
Real-time Systems Scheduling
Volume 1 – Fundamentals
Volume 2 – Focuses

DAVIM J. Paulo
Machinability of Advanced Materials

ESTAMPE Dominique
Supply Chain Performance and Evaluation Models

FAVRE Bernard
Introduction to Sustainable Transports

GAUTHIER Michaël, ANDREFF Nicolas, DOMBRE Etienne
Intracorporeal Robotics: From Milliscale to Nanoscale

MICOUIN Patrice
Model Based Systems Engineering: Fundamentals and Methods

MILLOT Patrick
Designing Human–Machine Cooperation Systems

NI Zhenjiang, PACORET Céline, BENOSMAN Ryad, RÉGNIER Stéphane
Haptic Feedback Teleoperation of Optical Tweezers

OUSTALOUP Alain
Diversity and Non-integer Differentiation for System Dynamics

REZG Nidhal, DELLAGI Sofien, KHATAD Abdelhakim
Joint Optimization of Maintenance and Production Policies

STEFANOIU Dan, BORNE Pierre, POPESCU Dumitru, FILIP Florin Gh., EL KAMEL Abdelkader
Optimization in Engineering Sciences: Metaheuristics, Stochastic Methods and Decision Support

2013

ALAZARD Daniel
Reverse Engineering in Control Design

ARIOUI Hichem, NEHAOUA Lamri
Driving Simulation

CHADLI Mohammed, COPPIER Hervé
Command-control for Real-time Systems

DAAFOUZ Jamal, TARBOURIECH Sophie, SIGALOTTI Mario
Hybrid Systems with Constraints

FEYEL Philippe
Loop-shaping Robust Control

FLAUS Jean-Marie
Risk Analysis: Socio-technical and Industrial Systems

FRIBOURG Laurent, SOULAT Romain
Control of Switching Systems by Invariance Analysis: Application to Power Electronics

GROSSARD Mathieu, RÉGNIER Stéphane, CHAILLET Nicolas
Flexible Robotics: Applications to Multiscale Manipulations

GRUNN Emmanuel, PHAM Anh Tuan
Modeling of Complex Systems: Application to Aeronautical Dynamics

HABIB Maki K., DAVIM J. Paulo
Interdisciplinary Mechatronics: Engineering Science and Research Development

HAMMADI Slim, KSOURI Mekki
Multimodal Transport Systems

JARBOUI Bassem, SIARRY Patrick, TEGHEM Jacques
Metaheuristics for Production Scheduling

KIRILLOV Oleg N., PELINOVSKY Dmitry E.
Nonlinear Physical Systems

LE Vu Tuan Hieu, STOICA Cristina, ALAMO Teodoro, CAMACHO Eduardo F., DUMUR Didier
Zonotopes: From Guaranteed State-estimation to Control

MACHADO Carolina, DAVIM J. Paulo
Management and Engineering Innovation

MORANA Joëlle
Sustainable Supply Chain Management

SANDOU Guillaume
Metaheuristic Optimization for the Design of Automatic Control Laws

STOICAN Florin, OLARU Sorin
Set-theoretic Fault Detection in Multisensor Systems

2012

Aït-Kadi Daoud, Chouinard Marc, Marcotte Suzanne, Riopel Diane
Sustainable Reverse Logistics Network: Engineering and Management

Borne Pierre, Popescu Dumitru, Filip Florin G., Stefanoiu Dan
Optimization in Engineering Sciences: Exact Methods

Chadli Mohammed, Borne Pierre
Multiple Models Approach in Automation: Takagi-Sugeno Fuzzy Systems

Davim J. Paulo
Lasers in Manufacturing

Declerck Philippe
Discrete Event Systems in Dioid Algebra and Conventional Algebra

Doumiati Moustapha, Charara Ali, Victorino Alessandro, Lechner Daniel
Vehicle Dynamics Estimation using Kalman Filtering: Experimental Validation

Guerrero José A, Lozano Rogelio
Flight Formation Control

Hammadi Slim, Ksouri Mekki
Advanced Mobility and Transport Engineering

Maillard Pierre
Competitive Quality Strategies

Matta Nada, Vandenboomgaerde Yves, Arlat Jean
Supervision and Safety of Complex Systems

Poler Raul *et al.*
Intelligent Non-hierarchical Manufacturing Networks

Troccaz Jocelyne
Medical Robotics

Yalaoui Alice, Chehade Hicham, Yalaoui Farouk, Amodeo Lionel
Optimization of Logistics

ZELM Martin *et al.*
Enterprise Interoperability –I-EASA12 Proceedings

2011

CANTOT Pascal, LUZEAUX Dominique
Simulation and Modeling of Systems of Systems

DAVIM J. Paulo
Mechatronics

DAVIM J. Paulo
Wood Machining

GROUS Ammar
Applied Metrology for Manufacturing Engineering

KOLSKI Christophe
Human–Computer Interactions in Transport

LUZEAUX Dominique, RUAULT Jean-René, WIPPLER Jean-Luc
Complex Systems and Systems of Systems Engineering

ZELM Martin, *et al.*
Enterprise Interoperability: IWEI2011 Proceedings

2010

BOTTA-GENOULAZ Valérie, CAMPAGNE Jean-Pierre, LLERENA Daniel, PELLEGRIN Claude
Supply Chain Performance: Collaboration, Alignment and Coordination

BOURLÈS Henri, GODFREY K.C. Kwan
Linear Systems

BOURRIÈRES Jean-Paul
Proceedings of CEISIE'09

CHAILLET Nicolas, REGNIER Stéphane
Microrobotics for Micromanipulation

DAVIM J. Paulo
Sustainable Manufacturing

GIORDANO Max, MATHIEU Luc, VILLENEUVE François
Product Life-Cycle Management: Geometric Variations

LOZANO Rogelio
Unmanned Aerial Vehicles: Embedded Control

LUZEAUX Dominique, RUAULT Jean-René
Systems of Systems

VILLENEUVE François, MATHIEU Luc
Geometric Tolerancing of Products

2009

DIAZ Michel
Petri Nets: Fundamental Models, Verification and Applications

OZEL Tugrul, DAVIM J. Paulo
Intelligent Machining

PITRAT Jacques
Artificial Beings

2008

ARTIGUES Christian, DEMASSEY Sophie, NÉRON Emmanuel
Resources–Constrained Project Scheduling

BILLAUT Jean-Charles, MOUKRIM Aziz, SANLAVILLE Eric
Flexibility and Robustness in Scheduling

DOCHAIN Denis
Bioprocess Control

LOPEZ Pierre, ROUBELLAT François
Production Scheduling

THIERRY Caroline, THOMAS André, BEL Gérard
Supply Chain Simulation and Management

2007

DE LARMINAT Philippe
Analysis and Control of Linear Systems

DOMBRE Etienne, KHALIL Wisama
Robot Manipulators

LAMNABHI Françoise *et al.*
Taming Heterogeneity and Complexity of Embedded Control

LIMNIOS Nikolaos
Fault Trees

2006

FRENCH COLLEGE OF METROLOGY
Metrology in Industry

NAJIM Kaddour
Control of Continuous Linear Systems